David and Amanda Erickson offer a groundbreaking parenting resource. The insightful strategies and practical advice in *The Flourishing Family* will help parents foster deeper connections, nurture their children's individual growth, and create a Christ-centered home. These words will breathe life and hope into parents longing for a better way to disciple their children.

HEATHER MacFADYEN
Host of the *Don't Mom Alone* podcast and author of *Right Where You Belong* and *Don't Mom Alone*

Say goodbye to fear-based parenting that requires instant obedience, sending parents and kids into an endless power struggle. Say hello to peaceful, purposeful, kind parenting that guides children's inner character, not just their outer behavior. *The Flourishing Family* will give parents back their confidence when it comes to connecting with their kids and raising them well. *This is the parenting book the evangelical world needs!*

SHEILA WRAY GREGOIRE
Founder of BareMarriage.com and coauthor of *She Deserves Better*

David and Amanda Erickson pour deep biblical knowledge, sharp theological acumen, and great human wisdom into this excellent guide for parents. While I expected a thoughtful and engaging text, I was elated to find also an inspiring spiritual maturity. Most importantly, the Ericksons remind us that a dynamic personal relationship with Jesus is the key to a blessed family. Take up, read, and grow into Christ with your children.

MALCOLM B. YARNELL III
Research professor of theology, Southwestern Baptist Theological Seminary, Fort Worth, and author of *God the Trinity*, *Special Revelation and Scripture*, and *The Formation of Christian Doctrine*

Perhaps if more adults represented Jesus in ~~this way through their~~ parenting, more children would be runnin~~g~~ rather than away from it as they grow olde~~r~~

profoundly healing—and practical—for all who want to lead
their families with Christlike love.

SARAH R. MOORE
Author of *Peaceful Discipline*, certified positive parenting coach, and
chairperson of the board for the American Society for the Positive Care
of Children

I wish I'd had this book while raising my young children. It is full
of grace and practical techniques, offering parents the freedom
to use gentle but firm practices to actually shape a child's heart.
I have learned so much from these authors and wish there were
more books like this to help parents navigate harmful disciplinary
advice that is prevalent even in Christian circles.

JAMI NATO
Author and entrepreneur

In these pages of testimony, you will read of David and Amanda's
personal journey toward a perspective change on parenting, one
that is based in Scripture and that reinforces discipline, excludes
punishment, and depends on love leading to true development.
If you are a young parent seeking credible and loving ways to
discipline your child, this book is for you.

JASON CURRY
President of Texas Baptist Home for Children

The Flourishing Family offers great theological reflection for
parents and is packed with practical insights and long-range
parenting studies set within the context of a personal parenting
journey. Trade in the rod for better (and far more biblical)
parenting. A must-read for Christian parents!

WILLIAM J. WEBB
Adjunct professor of biblical studies, Tyndale University, Toronto, and
author of *Corporal Punishment in the Bible*

A JESUS-CENTERED GUIDE TO PARENTING
WITH PEACE AND PURPOSE

The Flourishing Family

DR. DAVID AND AMANDA ERICKSON

TYNDALE
REFRESH®

Think Well. Live Well. Be Well.

Visit Tyndale online at tyndale.com.

Visit Tyndale Refresh online at tyndalerefresh.com.

Visit David and Amanda at flourishinghomesandfamilies.com.

Tyndale, Tyndale's quill logo, *Tyndale Refresh*, and the Tyndale Refresh logo are registered trademarks of Tyndale House Ministries. Tyndale Refresh is a nonfiction imprint of Tyndale House Publishers, Carol Stream, Illinois.

The Flourishing Family: A Jesus-Centered Guide to Parenting with Peace and Purpose

Cover designed by Sarah Susan Richardson

Published in association with Jenni Burke of Illuminate Literary Agency: www.illuminateliterary.com.

The URLs in this book were verified prior to publication. The publisher is not responsible for content in the links, links that have expired, or websites that have changed ownership after that time.

For information about special discounts for bulk purchases, please contact Tyndale House Publishers at csresponse@tyndale.com, or call 1-855-277-9400.

Library of Congress Cataloging-in-Publication Data

A catalog record for this book is available from the Library of Congress.

ISBN 978-1-4964-8846-6

Printed in the United States of America

30	29	28	27	26	25	24
7	6	5	4	3	2	1

For Ezra and Elijah.

From your earliest days we have prayed that you will be mighty men of courage who walk in the way of Jesus and who proclaim mercy and truth to the nations. Being your mama and daddy is the greatest privilege and adventure of our lives, and this front-row seat that allows us to watch you both be and grow into who God made you to be is the absolute best. May the Lord bless you and keep you, and make His face shine upon you, and give you peace.

Contents

Foreword

by Jim and Lynne Jackson

We entered parenthood in 1987 with great delight! Having been ministry leaders and professionals working with children, we thought our skills with other people's kids would equip us well. But our three intense kids, born in a four-year span, challenged us beyond our wildest imagination.

Nothing equipped us for the steady rise of confusion, chaos, and conflict we faced daily in our own home. In our desperation to love our kids well, raise them "in the training and instruction of the Lord" (Ephesians 6:4), and establish some order, we sought help from many of the go-to Christian parenting resources of the day. Nearly all of them offered appealing formulas for child-rearing that we were told would produce obedient, responsible children if we followed them consistently.

Something—either the formulas or our ability for consistency—was lacking. The A + B = C equation for gaining immediate obedience and respect from our children was resulting in little of either and was costing us connection with them. We frequently found ourselves caught between the impulse to "be the parent" (firmly demand desired behavior) and the longing to exemplify God's mercy, grace, and love with our beloved offspring. Doing both didn't seem possible.

Oh, to have had *The Flourishing Family* back then!

We became more discouraged and unsettled. How could we demand respect when we often subtly disrespected each other or our children? How could we expect quick obedience when we ourselves were frequently disobedient to the command to love God and each other? Why should we address specks in our kids' eyes when we had logs (of anxiety, condescension, and resentment) in our own (see Matthew 7:3-5, NLT)?

Our son, wise beyond his five years, bluntly pointed out one of those logs one day when we spanked him for aggression toward his sister. "When you hit me because I hit her, what does that *teach* me?" Telling him, "Don't hit your sister anymore" didn't feel honest when we knew the power of modeling. And justifying our action with "the Bible commands it" when we were so deeply conflicted also didn't seem honest. If we *were* truthful, we might have admitted, "It gives us a sense of control."

As our children grew, our love deepened, as did our discomfort. These were full-blown humans, worthy of all the Bible's "one another" commands.

I (Jim) sought wisdom from a highly recommended parenting book. It implored me to command obedience, citing Ephesians 6:1-3, which begins "Children, obey your parents. . . ." It then listed method upon method for disciplining (punishing) children so they would someday become obedient, respectful, God-fearing, responsible humans.

It occurred to me that *these verses were not even meant for parents*! They were directed to *children*. It's the Holy Spirit's job to teach my child their meaning. Could it be that the passage's application for us was to treat our kids so they would trust us enough to obey?

Then came the parents' directive in 6:4: "Fathers, do not exasperate your children" (NIV). The book lightly addressed this by suggesting that kids get exasperated if they're allowed to misbehave. It then doubled down on the second part of the verse: "but bring them up in the training and instruction of the Lord," which the writer equated with disciplining by using a pain-inflicting object. That sounded pretty exasperating to me.

I wondered to myself, *Why do Christian parenting "experts" not suggest that punishing kids a lot might just exasperate them, or even that our punishment of children might be rooted in our own sinful need for control? Why don't they talk more about how to uphold the image of God in our kids?* God's grace and mercy were nowhere in sight.

When I (Lynne) first searched the Bible for new insight and clear commands to parents, I was disappointed and frustrated. Then one day I read 1 Thessalonians 2. Paul, who called himself a spiritual "father through the gospel" to those he discipled (1 Corinthians 4:15, NIV), described a remarkable parent-child relationship with the Thessalonian believers. His role was to be as gentle as a nursing mother and as supportive as a father who encourages, comforts, and urges his children to live lives worthy of God. Nothing in this passage suggested that Paul was demanding, punitive, harsh, or controlling with his "children."

I was giddy with joy! We could now look to the example of Paul and, of course, Jesus who "parented" His rather unruly (prone to "sibling conflict") disciples. This became our guiding paradigm for parenting. And we began to recognize the gentleness, encouragement, and comfort our Father has for *us* in our everyday struggles.

On the one hand, our search was over, but on the other hand, it had just started. We began to focus on keeping our hearts connected to our kids, while we nurtured the "wisdom of the righteous" (Luke 1:17, NIV) to guide them away from disobedience. What we learned led us to launch Connected Families in 2002 in order to equip parents with encouraging, practical, and soul-filling resources for bringing God's life-giving grace and truth into Christian homes.

How we wish we'd had allies like Flourishing Homes & Families and the book you are about to read then! David and Amanda Erickson have built a ministry that would surely have been our lifeline back in the day. These beloved colaborers combine robust theological rigor and wisdom with concrete practicality. And it turns out (as you'll read) that the idea of parenting gently is not a new idea. In these pages you will discover solid evidence for a graceful, nonpunitive way to parent that is undergirded by *biblical, historically faithful* Christian teaching.

In this treasure of a book you'll find great encouragement and a compelling case for rethinking your parenting journey. May your learning be accelerated at a time and place in history when our world needs families who flourish in God's grace and truth more than ever before!

From Frantic to Flourishing

David and I realized something was terribly wrong one afternoon when I had a panic attack at the grocery store after church. The store was bursting with people; the lines were long and my patience was short. Although I was dressed in my Sunday best, I was about to spiral into one of the worst anxiety attacks I'd had as a parent. And my kids weren't even with me.

After what felt like forever, it was finally my turn to check out, and I placed the items onto the belt with expert speed and efficiency. Zoning out to the rhythmic noise of the scanner, I missed the debit machine beeping at me and almost didn't hear the cashier beckon for my attention.

"Um, ma'am?" she said again. "It looks like your debit card has been declined. Do you have another card we can try?"

Heat flushed my cheeks; surely the card reader was broken

or the cashier had made a mistake. Even though I knew I had adequate money in my account—even though I knew that I had another card to use in this type of emergency—my mind started to race uncontrollably. Immediately, I arrived at the worst-case scenario: *What if this lady thinks I'm trying to steal this bag of groceries? What if she calls Child Protective Services and they say I can't take care of my babies so they take them away? How did I let this happen?*

Sitting in my car a few minutes later, I felt intense pressure on my chest as I struggled to breathe. It was supposed to have been a quick in-and-out trip for a couple of items, and in those few moments of what typically would have been a slight inconvenience, my mind had gone to a dark place. Without warning I had an overwhelming sense that someone else—anyone else—would be better at this mom thing than I was, and CPS was almost certainly going to think so. In spite of the hot tears streaming down my cheeks and blurring my vision, I drove home, sat down, cried out to God, and practically screamed at David, "I don't know what's wrong, but I need help! I can't do this anymore."

The *this* I was referring to was the constant weight of fear and dread that hovered over me like a cloud. After five years of infertility, a heartbreaking miscarriage, and then the birth of two rainbow babies seventeen months apart, I was overwhelmed by the responsibilities of caring for our home, feeding my family, crafting and creating with my children, and making sure they were socialized, well-mannered, and "on track" (whatever that means). Lest you forget, I also had to instill in them correct morals and values while overseeing their spiritual formation. And with two very young toddlers, keeping them safe felt like a full-time job all by itself—much less doing anything else!

Parenting felt like one of the biggest and most important callings of my life—and I felt completely and utterly lost. But while I first admitted something was wrong after that debilitating panic attack left me shaking in my car, I recognized that it was my uncontrollable anger and "mom rage" that showed up almost daily that got me there. Why did I—a mom who loved Jesus and my children dearly—so often let fear and uncertainty consume me, leading me to react with irritation and exasperation? How had I lost sight of what was most important to me as a parent? It was this journey through postpartum anxiety that led David and me to pursue true shalom—wholehearted, whole-person peace and flourishing—especially as it pertained to our parenting. Not just for us, but for our children as well.

When we set out to raise our children "in the nurture and admonition of the Lord" (Ephesians 6:4, KJV), we thought we knew what that looked like. We read all the Christian parenting books available to us; and as seminary graduates, we both knew the Bible inside and out. In addition, we had some experience, although our introduction to parenthood hadn't begun in the conventional way. A couple of years before our older son was born, we had been foster parents to three boys—two preteens and a teenager—so we knew how critical it was to build trust and establish loving limits with each child.

Even so, as our two boys grew into toddlerhood and parenting became more challenging, we began to notice a very real disconnect between our actions as parents and the biblical and theological principles we claimed were most important to us. The things we said we believed about God, grace, sin, repentance, and more didn't seem to line up with how we were trying to discipline our children. Somehow, even with all the resources available at our fingertips, we felt lost, unsure, and completely out of our depth.

When it came to parenting, we craved confidence, wisdom, and—most of all—peace. So we dove into the Bible and reexamined it without the blinders of our past assumptions and with a heart to truly understand what the Spirit had inspired. We began to build our parenting ideas on fundamental Christian theological principles—not merely a handful of proof texts whose interpretation we thought we knew—along with the latest developments in neuroscience and child psychology. The result was a new perspective—one that cultivated peace, gentleness, and confidence. One that enabled us to feel that our family was no longer simply surviving but flourishing in all that God had for us.

During our exploration, we met countless other parents on a journey quite similar to our own. Like us, they were convicted to pursue gentleness and peace in their parenting and were deeply committed to honoring and obeying Scripture in the process. In 2019, we founded Flourishing Homes & Families, more as a means by which to share our own spiritual and parenting journey than to establish ourselves as parenting experts. What started as vulnerably wrestling through postpartum anxiety and rage, sharing what helped our boys with certain tricky behaviors and what the Holy Spirit was revealing to us through deep study eventually grew to be a global ministry. Today, we are a community of parents committed to leading our families well using principles that are rooted in Jesus' teaching and backed by modern neuroscience. Through workshops and online and personal coaching, we've had the privilege to connect with thousands of families who are relentlessly pursuing peace and purpose in their families.

If you're anything like the moms and dads we interact with daily, you picked up this book because you're looking for solid, proven, and biblically sound parenting advice. We get it. We know your struggle because we've lived it!

You desperately need peace in the midst of chaos in your home. You pray for peace when your little one is tossed about by waves of emotions. You long for peace in your relationship with your child. But most days, peace feels like the furthest thing from your four walls. Peace feels impossible when you notice the watching eyes of others scrutinizing your parenting. It seems inaccessible at the end of the day when you know you could have done better and can't bear the guilt that comes with thinking about how you messed up. And it feels impractical when the stakes are so high; your child's heart, mind, and spirit are in your hands.

Could it be that we often struggle because we have resigned ourselves to keeping the peace at any cost rather than resting in the work of Jesus—the Prince of Peace—and allowing His life-giving presence to cultivate true peace in our homes? The fact is, many of us learned how to be peacekeepers but not how to be peacemakers. A peacekeeper desires to maintain peace by avoiding conflict. This can show up in every relationship, but in parenting, it may lead us to press for more control over our children—increasing demands and handing out punishments in order to keep the situation contained. Yet forcing children to act as if they are at peace does little to introduce them to true peace or help them find peace with us or one another. Peacekeeping leads other parents to gravitate toward permissiveness—giving in to demands or trying to avoid disappointment. But true peacemaking doesn't merely bypass conflict either.

In general, peacekeepers hate rocking the boat and wind up sacrificing their own inner peace or peace with others in order to keep a semblance of peace on the outside. Peacemakers, on the other hand, are willing to confront both the inner and outer chaos in order to establish true peace, first within themselves and then with others. In parenting, peacemaking requires us to engage conflict, power struggles, tension, and chaos head-on so that we can bring peace, and hopefully harmony, into difficult situations.

Like everything, parenting isn't one-size-fits-all. Each family's history and makeup is different, so our goal is to equip you with tools and resources to try with your individual children in your unique environment. As much as you may want it, there is no formula, framework, system, blueprint, or strategy to parenting that will *guarantee* your child will become a Jesus-loving, well-adjusted, respectful, healthy, successful adult in ten or twenty years. Ultimately, you cannot control who your children become, but you can control what kind of parents you are and how much Jesus your children see in you. While there is no magic trick to parenting, moving toward principles that align with the true character and values of Christ *will* change the way your family operates in the day-to-day as well as in the long-term. We believe that these foundational principles will help you become more faithful parents, living out your trust in Jesus—the Prince of Peace—as you engage in the adventure of a lifetime.

In these pages we want to come alongside you in that endeavor. We've intentionally structured *The Flourishing Family* in such a way that you can easily find practical suggestions and tips for common parenting struggles. But please don't just skip to that part. It's essential to start by creating a new foundation for who you are as parents; after all, your identity is in Christ, not in how well-behaved your children are. We'll begin in part 1 by rethinking common assumptions about what the Bible says about parenting and identifying how you can cultivate the inner peace needed to parent your children with the character and heart of Jesus. When you become the person Jesus calls you to be, you become the parent your child needs.

Then in part 2, we'll introduce core principles and practices so you can confidently put this Jesus-centered paradigm into action. We've included a number of personal stories to show you how our own parenting experiences have shaped us. Because we've learned so much from the Flourishing Homes & Families community, we also share a few stories inspired by our coaching calls. We've changed the names and some details to protect these families' privacy. At the end of each chapter, you'll find reflection questions designed to help you consider how you might apply peacemaking principles to your own parenting. While we typically work with parents whose kids are ages ten and younger, we believe that the peacemaking principles we unpack in this book can be helpful to anyone.

One word about parenting styles: Many experts categorize the four parenting approaches as authoritarian, authoritative, permissive, or neglectful. Research shows that authoritative parenting—firm, appropriate boundaries held by parents in a loving, nurturing, and responsive way—generally best prepares children to become self-reliant, kind, and curious adults.[1] While we ascribe to this parenting style, our goal isn't to create another unique approach or set of tools to file under the authoritative parenting heading. There are already a plethora of approaches and tools! Our goal is to align our parenting approach with the teaching of Jesus and keep our focus on Him and our identity in Him.

Parenting with gentleness and peace doesn't come from having the "right" answer for all of your parenting questions. You won't find it by having perfect discipline strategies or by memorizing parenting scripts. True peace—the peace we unpack in *The Flourishing Family*—comes from Jesus. In His wisdom and goodness, God chose the gift of parenthood to shape you into the image of His Son. Trust that He will meet you in this book. Trust that you are the right parent for your child. Trust that His peace can change your home from the inside out so that your home and family can flourish.

PART 1

It Starts with Us

1

A God-Sized View of Children

"Hey! That's mine! This one is yours. This is my side of the table! Stop it right *now!*"

Until that moment, our house had been relatively quiet; our boys were in their room pushing their little wooden trains down an elaborate and expertly designed wooden track. They were pretty young, and while their conflict resolution skills were lacking, their wooden-train-layout skills were quite impressive. As you can probably imagine, in a house with two toddlers, relative quiet was remarkably rare, and I was enjoying a brief reprieve while Amanda was in town running errands.

But then, without warning, that beautiful, peaceful quiet shattered.

Jolted into action, I leapt out of my chair—I did *not* like what I was hearing and knew from experience that an argument could escalate to blows quickly. My older son's tone was decidedly harsh toward his little brother, not the kind words that we'd been encouraging in our children. Anger started to rise in my chest, and as I bounded down the hall, my mind raced with everything I was going to say as soon as I got there: *You know better than this. How many times do I have to tell you? This isn't the way we treat others! You need to apologize right now!*

The truth hit me as soon as I got to the doorway.

The tone I heard coming from Ezra's tiny lips? It was my own. The words he'd just said? They were mine. The harsh words I'd just heard were remarkably similar to the words I was about to speak— and had spoken plenty of times before. How could I tell my kids to treat each other with kindness and respect if I was seemingly incapable of doing the same?

Standing in their bedroom doorway, I watched my two boisterous little boys with blond hair and blue eyes look up from their wooden trains to each other and then to me. I was reminded once again that if I wanted my children to navigate disagreements and disputes with kindness, respect, honor, and calm clarity, I first had to change how I spoke to them in the midst of chaos and conflict.

Model Parents

If parenting doesn't humble us, what will? It didn't take Amanda or me long to realize that our children are like tiny mirrors, reflecting back to us our own immaturity and weaknesses. Oh, they reflect good traits as well. Their remarkably creative train tracks were a reflection of the engineering and building they'd seen me do time and again. And their love for dance parties and their quick responsiveness to others who were hurting reflected what they'd seen in their mom. For better or for worse, our young children start out life with a God-given ability to mimic, mirror, and imitate their parents.

After my realization in the bedroom doorway that afternoon, the image in the mirror was crystal clear, and it told me that it was time to take a good, long look at my actual beliefs (and resulting actions) about who children were and how they should be treated.

As a Christian, following Jesus is *the* most important thing to me. So when I'm struggling to parent, I turn to the Bible for clarity. After all, as Christians, we should allow Jesus' life and teaching to directly impact the way we parent. Then again, turning to Jesus for parenting advice might seem unexpected. After all, He wasn't a parent! As far as we know, He never changed a baby, calmed a toddler tantrum, or spent a night rocking a teething child. Wouldn't skimming parenting books by experts, bookmarking blog posts, and taking screenshots of social media tips make more sense? What could this Jewish rabbi teach us about raising children that we couldn't find in the innumerable parenting resources available at our fingertips?

At the heart of parenting with peace and purpose is the source of our peace: Jesus Christ. When writing about the coming Messiah hundreds of years before Jesus' birth, the prophet Isaiah said that one of His names would be the "Prince of Peace" (Isaiah 9:6). Later, Isaiah explained that Christ's peace is available to all who have faith in Him: "You will keep the mind that is dependent on you in perfect peace, for it is trusting in you" (26:3). In order to parent from a posture of peacemaking and gentleness, we must look to Jesus, not just for parenting wisdom but as the very source of life-giving, heart-changing peace. We seek His teaching not for specific strategies or tactics but for a Kingdom mindset and heart that guides our relationships with our children.

Admittedly, parenting is not a central focus of the Gospels. The purpose of Jesus' life, teaching, death, and resurrection was not to teach us how to be perfect parents but instead to show us how to be His people made in His image. He also modeled how we should treat others and interact with those who don't agree with us. And while it may not be the most intuitive thing to try to apply His teaching and example to parenting, it was probably inevitable for a generation that was raised on WWJD—What Would Jesus Do?—to look to Him here as well.

When I (Amanda) was ten or eleven, my whole family memorized the Sermon on the Mount. We diligently learned and consistently practiced reciting Matthew 5, 6, and 7. I remember coming up with a trick for keeping the Beatitudes in order, and making a connection between Jesus' teaching about the testimony of bearing good (spiritual) fruit in Matthew 7:15-20 and Paul's description of Spirit-produced fruit in Galatians 5:22-26. Though I was only a kid, I was beginning to see that Jesus' life and teaching are just as important to Christian living as His death and resurrection. Looking back, I can see that memorizing and internalizing what is perhaps His most famous teaching at such a young age had a profound impact on me. Little did I know that early in my parenting journey Jesus' teaching on the Kingdom of Heaven would be foundational in cultivating a family culture in our home.

As we read the Gospels with an eye for how we might apply Jesus' teaching to parenting, we find that the way we view children matters to Jesus. And whether we're aware of it or not, how we treat children directly reflects the way we view them.

Jesus Loves the Little Children

Have you ever found yourself impatiently nudging your kids toward the car while trying to make a getaway from the park, only to get distracted by a last-minute conversation with a neighbor after your kiddos are finally buckled in? It can be easy to take the position that children are less important or less worthy of respect because they are smaller, less capable, less mature, and less emotionally controlled. While most people will not put it in such blunt terms, this is the dominant view of our culture—children are not worthy of the same respect or treatment as adults.

But that's not Jesus' view. Just because children are lesser in the eyes of the world does not make them less valuable in the eyes of God. The Bible records one surefire way to make Jesus angry with His followers—treat children as less important than adults.

Now Jesus wasn't a particularly angry man. Yes, on a few occasions he became irate with the hardness of people's hearts, the blindness of the religious leaders, or the mercenary priesthood in the Temple. Jesus is righteous, and that righteousness includes a holy anger directed at those who are harming others and leading them astray. But these are rare moments in a life primarily marked by patience and gentleness.

And yet in Mark 10:13-16 we read about parents bringing their children to see Jesus while He was teaching. In the previous verses Jesus had been having an advanced, technical discussion with religious leaders and later with His disciples about when Scripture permits divorce. The disciples saw these families as an interruption and attempted to shoo the children away from important adult conversations.

There was just one problem: Jesus wasn't having it.

Seeing His disciples dismiss the children made Jesus *really* furious. In fact, this is the only time the Gospels explicitly describe Jesus as being angry with His own disciples. To be fair, there are a few places where we, as readers, often perceive the words of Jesus to His disciples as originating in anger. (It's not hard to imagine "Get behind me, Satan!" [Matthew 16:23] being said with hostility.) In reality, much of that perception is grounded in exactly that: perception. It's our interpretation of the interaction, deduced from the words of the Gospels. But Mark 10:14 is different. In this one instance, Mark leaves us no doubt: He tells us Jesus was *indignant* with the disciples.[1]

We have zero indication that the disciples were truly mistreating these children. They weren't abusing them; they were simply doing what their culture expected of them. They treated the children as less important than the other people present, elevating the status, expectations, and interests of adults over the children's needs. In the first century, children were considered insignificant and unimportant. They had very little value. So it would not have been surprising or unexpected for the disciples to send them away.[2]

But Jesus wasn't interested in cultural expectations. His Kingdom is a "last will be first" and for "the least of these" kind of Kingdom.[3] This was His consistent message. Yet when given the opportunity to put it into practice, the disciples missed the mark.

Like the disciples, we can learn from this interaction. Until we are willing to see our children as who God made them to be, we will never treat them the way God calls us to. If our first thought about our children is that they are a hassle or manipulative, we are not seeing them as God does. We can acknowledge the challenges of raising children while still recognizing that they are made in God's image and profoundly loved by Him.

This is heart work. Jesus-centered parenting welcomes our children, blesses them, and regards them as important. More than anything, it honors the divine image in them. It is only when we begin to grasp the deep, profound love that God has for our children that we can see them as they wholly are. It is then that we can balance their struggles and failures with the reality of who they are: image bearers of Almighty God. If we see them as less than this, we are quick to coerce and manipulate them. When we see them as image bearers, we are able to treat them with respect and dignity.

The Real Treasure

Whether by a stroke of luck or incessant prevention on our part, somehow David and I managed to make it through the toddler and preschool years without any coloring on the walls or furniture. Naturally, we thought we were in the clear, and for a few years crayons, markers, and pencils stayed neatly in their arts and crafts spot on the shelf, easily accessible to busy, creative little hands.

That all changed when our youngest was in first grade. Yes, you read that correctly, and to be sure, we were as surprised as you may be. Because we'd kept all writing utensils out of reach when our children were small, we'd never had an actual conversation about keeping art on paper, not the walls. By the time Elijah was in first grade, it had completely escaped us that maybe we should have a chat about our expectations for artistic expression.

One night just before bedtime I was sitting on the boys' bedroom floor talking with Elijah while he got into his pajamas. We were following our normal bedtime routine: lights low, soft voices, steady movement toward being ready to snuggle and read before lights out. As we talked, Elijah pointed at the bottom drawer of the boys' dresser. "Mommy, look! It's a smiley face!" he said with so much pride and excitement, watching me closely to see my reaction.

In a split second I felt the gentle nudging of the Holy Spirit in my heart. See, Elijah hadn't drawn on the cheap plastic shelves in their closet or the easily replaceable furniture elsewhere in their room. No, he had etched a tiny smiley face on a sturdy, well-made chest of drawers that's been in the family for generations. That was his chosen canvas.

If this had happened earlier in our parenting, I would almost surely have lost it. And if not lost it completely, I know I would have reacted very sternly by "laying down the law." But this was many years into purposefully pursuing peace and gentleness with our children. I instinctively knew I had a choice in how I reacted, and the stakes were high: My response would reveal to my son which was more important, him or the family heirloom.

Reading that on paper in black and white, the "right choice" in this moment seems clear: Of course my child is more valuable than treasured furniture that had been passed down to me. And yet standing there in the heat of the moment looking at this well-loved antique that had just been damaged, it would have been easy to send an unintended message that the antique dresser was more important than my child.

If we're going to be able to face such situations with supernatural peace, we must have a foundational understanding of *why* children are so valuable. They are so treasured and loved by God because they are made in *His* image. To understand that, we have to go all the way back to the beginning of creation.

Imaging God

Genesis 1 is the biblical account of the creation of the world. If you're familiar with it, you know the story is divided into seven days and carefully constructed to emphasize various aspects of God's creative work. Through the carefully designed literary patterns found in the seven days of the story, a couple of things stand out.[4] They're intended to draw our attention because they are important concepts that are vital for our understanding of this world.

One remarkable part of Genesis 1 is the description of the creation of humans. From a literary perspective, it doesn't quite fit with the structure of the narrative, and that's not because it's an afterthought. It stands out as an intentional and thoughtful way to highlight the brilliance and uniqueness of this part of the story. It's designed to captivate our attention! Ancient readers and listeners would have been equally captivated. Every primeval culture had a creation story about how their god created the world. The details vary quite a lot from culture to culture, and there are as many differences with the Genesis account as there are similarities. Yet ancient Syrians or Egyptians would have found Israel's account of creation somewhat familiar—until, that is, God starts talking about humans.

The stunning, breathtaking claim of Genesis 1 is that all humans are made in the image of God. In some ways, we've gotten so accustomed to the idea of human equality that we forget how utterly revolutionary this claim would have been to the ancient world. Sure, plenty of cultures included the idea of a human made in the image of their god or gods as part of their creation story— often only the king bore the divine image and was thought to be an earthly representative of god, such as in ancient Egypt where the pharaoh was considered an image of Ra, the sun god. Some cultures extended the divine image to include more than one man, but it was always a very select group. This exclusivity was a tool used by rulers to subjugate the masses, giving those who bore the image of god justification for oppressing and exploiting those who did not.[5]

The God of Israel reveals a completely different reality for humanity. The God who later calls His people to be set apart, sets Himself apart in His creation narrative by declaring that all humans are made in His image. With this He declares that we are not *designed* to be oppressors and oppressed, masters and slaves, or kings and subjects. Instead, we are all made to be bearers of the divine image; reflections of His divine nature in this created world. And God clarifies that it is not just men who are image bearers, but women equally bear the divine image (Genesis 1:27). Every person is made in the image of God. It really is that simple. And it is as stunning in today's culture as it was in the ancient world.

JESUS, THE IMAGE OF GOD

While Genesis 1 is clear that humans are made in God's image, imme-diately after the entrance of sin into the world, Genesis records the many ways humans begin to reject that truth and live in opposition to it. Ultimately God enters into His own creation through Jesus' coming, not just as God in a human body, but as both fully human and fully God. He is the ultimate image of God, showing us not only who God is (John 1:18; Colossians 1:15) but demonstrating what true, untainted humanity is like.

As God become man, Jesus does not just redeem people from their sin, but He shows us how to live as those made in God's image. When we pursue the Jesus-centered life, we are living in the fullness of our humanity as we are transformed by the power of the Spirit into conformity with the image of God in Christ (Romans 8:29; Colossians 3:10). Parenting with the goal of honoring the image of God in our children may be counterintuitive to the world, but it's part of living the Jesus-transformed life.[6]

When this foundational concept is combined with passages like Psalm 139 and Jeremiah 1, it becomes beautifully clear: From the womb onward, *every* person is made in the image of God. Strong or weak, old or young, healthy or disabled, neurodiverse or neuro-typical. The child born with such severe disabilities that they will never take a step bears the divine image just as much as the athlete who sets world records climbing Mount Everest. Not even sin can erase the image of God in us; when Adam and Eve later fall into sin (Genesis 3), they continue to carry the image of God as human beings (Genesis 9:6, James 3:9). This is at the core of who we are, foundational to our understanding of what it means to be human.

Unexpected Treasure

When our artistically inclined son took his creativity and artistic prowess to that chest of drawers, recognizing his inherent worth and dignity helped me (Amanda) keep perspective so that I could respond with grace and kindness.

"I see that smiley face; it's so small!" I squeaked, trying to control my tone. It was little; I probably wouldn't have noticed it if he hadn't pointed it out. But it didn't feel small. "Can you tell me about it?" I asked, genuinely curious. I could have said (and, truthfully, a part of me *wanted* to say), "What were you thinking? You know better than this!" But my desire to nurture his heart and treat him with respect changed everything.

"I drew it with a pencil the other day!" he said. That explained why it was slightly etched into the wood.

"You drew a smiley face on your drawer the other day," I said, echoing his words. "And you seem pleased with it. You're always very proud of your art." (It should be said that Elijah really is a gifted artist, and he has every right to be proud of his ability.)

"Yes!" he said. He was still smiling with such satisfaction. I tried to put myself in his shoes: Carving is no small skill, and he truly used remarkable precision in etching that face.

I took a breath and gave him a soft smile. "Thank you for showing me your art, Elijah. Your art is so important to me. I'm surprised you drew on the drawer, though. I'm curious about that."

He looked at me, confused. "Oh, that's because I didn't have any paper in here," he said, as if he was stating the obvious. Of course. While not the most mature or informed decision, I had to admit that coming up with an alternative canvas was not entirely unreasonable.

"I see. You know what, your art is important to me; it's why we have so many pictures hung up and saved. You decided it was time to draw, but you didn't have any paper—that makes sense! I don't think we can hang this up, though, because it's not on paper. Hmmm!" I could tell that I had his attention and that he was following every word I said.

I shifted my tone from curious to slightly more serious, trying to shy away from being harsh or shaming. "You know, these drawers are special too. Did you know they belonged to my grandma and grandpa?" Elijah's eyes got big, a new connection and understanding dawning. He shook his head and looked at his smiley face.

"Here's the thing, bud," I said, a hand on his shoulder. "You know your art is special to me. But these drawers are special to me too. And they were not meant to be special together. Where does your art belong?"

Elijah's exuberant pride had turned to quiet introspection (or at least whatever a seven-year-old can muster late in the day when he's less than an hour from being asleep). He looked at me and then at the drawer. "Paper," he said quietly.

"You're right. And now that I know you know this, that's where I expect it to stay. If you want to practice carving or etching on wood, we can find a way for you to do that with wood that hasn't been made into furniture. For now, we're going to keep pencils on the art shelf, not in your room. And I'll work on making sure there's paper there, too, so that whenever you want to draw, you have everything you need."

The whole conversation was only a couple of minutes, and in that time, David popped his head in twice to see what was going on. Bedtime rarely takes such a serious tone. But as he peeked around the door, I glanced at him and gave a gentle nod. This situation was under control, I was under control, and the opportunity for peaceful and purposeful correction wasn't missed.

I can honestly say that my family heirloom is even more precious to me now. Not because I *wanted* a tiny smiley face in the bottom right corner of the bottom drawer, but because I was able to navigate that conflict with Elijah with peace and purpose, gentleness and grace. It's now a beautiful reminder of how far we've come.

The Golden Rule

In Matthew 7:12, Jesus gives the crowning principle, the gold standard of how we should be in the world as His followers: We are to treat others as we want to be treated.

Our children don't arrive in this world treating us (their life-giving, good-gift-bearing parents) the way we want to be treated. From toddlerhood to the teenage years, kids generally don't show their parents all the respect, love, and appreciation we would hope for. Even though we know children learn honor, obedience, and wisdom slowly, it can be tempting to decide that we're going to demand deference from children while not showing any consideration to them. Jesus firmly rejects such parental hypocrisy.

Whatever we want our children to do and be starts with us. We have to do to our children the things we want them to do to us and others. We have to speak to our children the words we want them to speak to us and others. We must model to our children the ways we want them to listen to and be mindful of us and others. If that feels counterintuitive to you, you're not alone! After all, we are bigger and wiser. Why shouldn't we leverage that power over our children while we still have it? But is that how we want others to treat us? Is that how Jesus teaches us to use authority when we have it?

It isn't. Fundamentally, our children are people. And Christ's commands about how to treat people apply to them just as much as to anyone else.

It's simple to say but sometimes so very hard to do. Consider what Jesus says in the Sermon on the Mount:

> Who among you, if his son asks him for bread, will
> give him a stone? Or if he asks for a fish, will give him a

snake? If you then, who are evil, know how to give good gifts to your children, how much more will your Father in heaven give good things to those who ask him. Therefore, whatever you want others to do for you, do also the same for them, for this is the Law and the Prophets.

MATTHEW 7:9-12

And God's greatest gift to us? Jesus. When we think about the messianic hope that is fulfilled in Jesus, we often narrow in on the eternal salvation provided through Jesus' death, burial, and resurrection. But the good news of Jesus cannot be confined to a hope for a heavenly future. Jesus was sent by God not only to save His people from condemnation but also to establish a Kingdom of those whose hearts have been renewed by His grace and to transform our way of living. And that includes our parenting.

Growth > Guilt

I (David) wish I could tell you that, after the Toy Train Kerfuffle, I never spoke harshly to either of my sons again. I wish I could tell you that I have succeeded in treating them with honor and dignity and the love of Christ a full 100 percent of the time. But I can't.

THINGS TO TELL MYSELF WHEN I MAKE A PARENTING MISTAKE

- With each mistake, I discover opportunities for growth, allowing God's forgiveness to shape my path as a parent.
- My child doesn't need me to be perfect; they need me to learn from my mistakes and to repair and restore our relationship.
- I accept God's gentleness and grace toward me, knowing His strength is made perfect in my weaknesses.

God intends for parents to meet the needs of their children, yet even the most devoted parents fail their children sometimes. It is natural and normal to grieve and lament past choices and actions. Guilt, regret, and remorse are not only typical and healthy responses; they also serve to direct us toward progress and maturity. The fact that you are reading this book is proof that you are committed to that growth.

You are a *great* parent. And, just like every other great parent, you've made mistakes. As you continue on this journey, resist the urge to fall into negative self-talk (*I'm a horrible parent!*), make absolute statements (*I've ruined my relationship with my child*), or try to shame yourself into being a better parent (*If I don't get this right from now on, I'm probably not going to have a good relationship with my kids as adults*). Remember, your children don't need a perfect parent in order to flourish and thrive. They need *you*. They need a parent who is present, who is always learning and growing, and who diligently works to repair, restore, and strengthen the trust-based parent-child relationship.

You haven't failed, and you are not failing. You are, and always have been, *becoming* the parent Christ has called you to be.

Reflection Questions

1. In light of your journey toward a new parenting paradigm, what are the core values and aspirations you hold for your own parenting? How do these ideals align with the concept of viewing children as image bearers of God?

2. Reflect on a recent parenting challenge where you responded in a way you later regretted. How can you apply the principle of choosing "growth over guilt" in this situation? What steps can you take to learn from the experience and grow as a parent?

3. Can you recall an instance from your upbringing in which your parents' actions toward you failed to demonstrate your inherent worth as an image bearer of God? How does this memory fuel your commitment to parent differently and instill a sense of respect and dignity in your own children?

4. How can you strike a balance between reflecting on your own childhood experiences and actively engaging in intentional parenting practices? What practical steps can you take to translate your reflections into positive actions that align with your aspirations for parenting?

2

The Power of Abiding

When I was pregnant with our second son, Elijah, David's mom suffered a tragic accident while on vacation in Switzerland. We got the call that Fourth of July weekend. I remember the sadness and fear in my father-in-law's voice as he told us that Mom was in a coma and had been airlifted to the hospital. The next several weeks were excruciating.

Being five months pregnant, I was a little more emotional than the rest of the family. I was also battling perinatal anxiety; I just didn't know it yet. I did my best to hold it together for fifteen-month-old Ezra, who was just starting to walk. Mom's injury was severe, and the Swiss doctors warned us that she might have life-altering limitations as a result of the accident. When she took longer than anticipated to come out of the coma, we started entertaining a barrage of what-if questions. Among all of our legitimate worries and concerns for her life, I remember having an irrational fear that Ezra would be our only baby with a crocheted blanket from his grammy. Our second baby wouldn't have that special, made-with-love treasure.

David's mom made a miraculous recovery. She still lives with the effects of traumatic brain injury, but our deepest fears never came to fruition. When Elijah was born a few months later, she made the twelve-hour drive to our house to help us. Perhaps the memory I treasure most from her visit: She brought Elijah's freshly crocheted blanket with her. We are so thankful for her testimony of healing.

Three years later, my phone lit up with texts in the middle of the night. My mom had suffered a heart attack. I immediately called my dad for an update. He told me that she was being flown via Life Flight from our tiny local hospital to the cardiac unit of a hospital about an hour north. My dad had raced the fifty miles to that hospital, but when he arrived, Mom wasn't there. No helicopter, no Mom. Something had gone wrong.

Lying in bed that night, I found myself resting in so much peace—an inner peace I did not have when my mother-in-law's life hung in the balance three years before. Since her accident I had been in counseling and had begun to develop the skills and tools to cope with anxiety and fear. This time around, I was able to feel the fear of uncertainty without spiraling into irrational anxiety. And throughout the night I clung to one verse that shifted everything for me: "You will keep the mind that is dependent on you in perfect peace, for it is trusting in you" (Isaiah 26:3).

God's Spirit brought that verse to my mind in the dark, uncertain hours as I waited for an update about my mama. Each time my mind wandered into the what-ifs and the unknown, I chose to dwell on the goodness of God. I started by making a mental list of how I see His goodness and faithfulness in Scripture—how He proved faithful when every one of His human ambassadors proved faithless. Next I reflected on how we see His goodness and faithfulness in nature—how the birds of the air and the flowers of the field do not worry or wilt but are sustained by the resplendent and gracious love of God (Matthew 6:25-34). And then I anchored myself to all the ways God's goodness and faithfulness were evident in my own life—His patient pursuit of my heart through years of infertility, His abundant provision through His people when we became foster parents, and the many good gifts we enjoy daily.

The emotional storm I experienced that night wasn't easy or enjoyable. But it was peaceable—because I anchored myself to the Prince of Peace and rested securely in Him. And the glorious truth I learned was this: I cannot control every situation, and I cannot always control my emotions; but I can control my response to situations, and with much work and intention, I can control what I do with heavy emotions. As I discovered after Elijah's birth, new babies, hormones, and stress still threaten to overwhelm me. Thankfully, God is not burdened or disoriented by my overwhelm, and looking back, I can see how He has faithfully carried our family through tumultuous storms.

The helicopter carrying my mom did eventually show up at the hospital that night. She had a successful emergency procedure, and forty-eight hours later she was home. Her recovery was remarkable. Years later, David and I have front-row seats as our boys develop relationships with both of their grandmas, and we see what a gift they each are to one another. We also have a keen awareness of how little control we actually have—over life-threatening situations, as well as over our children and their behavior.

Our Safe Place

One of the fundamental differences between those two frightening experiences with our mothers was that by the time the second one occurred, we had already learned how futile it is to grasp for control. Releasing our need to be in charge of as many details of our life as possible gave us freedom to rest and abide in Jesus. Of course, that's what we all hope our children will do with us, right? Stop fighting for control and just trust our wisdom and faithfulness! It doesn't quite work that way, though, does it?

The truth is, we will never attain the goals of Christian parenting if we only focus on trying to control our children and their behavior—doing everything we can to keep them safe and compliant. In fact, when we put Jesus at the center of our parenting, He leads us to put more focus on His refining and equipping work in *us*.

How does Jesus' teaching inform and define our role as parents? Let's take a quick look at the opening lines of the most famous sermon He ever preached. The Sermon on the Mount opens with a series of short sayings called the Beatitudes, including this one:

> Blessed are the peacemakers,
> for they will be called sons of God.
> MATTHEW 5:9

Being a peacemaker can feel nearly impossible at times, we know. Sleepless nights with a teething baby, toddler tantrums over the wrong-colored sippy cup, and siblings learning complex social dynamics with each other often lead to feelings of chaos and friction rather than peace and harmony. Our living rooms become wrestling rings to which we are unwilling referees. We feel as if we should strap on a blue helmet like a UN peacekeeper when we get in the car to enforce the demilitarized zone in the back seat.

It's in these moments when our children push us to the brink that we see how desperately *we* need the work of the Holy Spirit in us. It is only through Him that we can find real peace—the kind that allows us to be peacemakers when our children are anything but peaceful. Parenting as peacemakers helps our children learn how to problem-solve, how to reconcile, and how to restore relationship.

But we can model this only by cultivating peace within our own hearts first, leaning into the power of the Holy Spirit and hiding ourselves in the safe harbor of Jesus' peace. This is where our own inner strength is galvanized.

I (David) used to think that some people are peace-filled and some simply are not. Some are just fortunate to have a personality and temperament that lends itself to peace and patience. I even thought I was one of the lucky ones! Until I became a parent. While I had little trouble being a peaceful presence at work, at church, and in many relationships, small children have a way of testing the true limits of our peace and patience. My children forced me to confront the reality that while I might have a more chill personality than many others, I still needed to tap into a source of peace much bigger than myself.

It isn't all that surprising. Parenting brings into spectacularly clear focus everything we cannot control, no matter how much we wish we could. And maintaining peace when so many things are outside our control can seem unattainable. Peace while my toddler is melting down in the middle of the cereal aisle? Peace when the preschool calls me to pick up my child because he bit three kids? Peace when everybody is hungry, my kids are passing the time by annoying each other as much as possible, and I can't get two uninterrupted minutes in the kitchen? Life as a parent certainly isn't an endless string of peaceful moments of meditation. It's more like a long list of all the moments and things I cannot control.

Yet it is exactly this mundane chaos of life into which Jesus stepped and boldly declared, "My peace I give to you" (John 14:27). The peace we need comes from Jesus. He stepped into the mayhem and confusion of this world, right into the middle of the political upheaval, oppression, spiritual poverty, and "peace" through domination that was the Pax Romana.[1] As He drew people to Himself, Jesus consistently offered them peace—the fulfillment of God's shalom—in the midst of chaos. And that same divinely inspired peace *is* available to us.

Jesus is the source of peace we bring to our home and families. He speaks to this in John 15, where He beautifully describes us as branches that bear fruit when we are connected to the Vine. We are united with Christ in our salvation, but Jesus also speaks about how our continuing to remain in Him leads to spiritual fruit. That is, there is more to being a follower of Jesus, and parenting as a follower of Jesus, than a prayer or a moment of faith. It is an ongoing, day-by-day abiding in Him.

If you're like us, you might be looking for a helpful checklist of what it means to abide in Christ. Perhaps, if such a list existed, we'd expect to find things like read the Bible more, pray more, and serve in the church more. While a helpful list might seem tempting, the difficult truth is that these expectations often lead us to feeling like we need to try harder to be better Christians—and in our case, better Christian parents.

But that's not what abiding in Christ is. Not that the Bible, prayer, and church aren't important or have no relevance to our relationship with Jesus. But "do more, try harder" is not the answer. This is especially true in some of the more intense or challenging seasons of parenting.

Not long before he died, well-known New York City pastor Tim Keller described his extensive daily quiet-time routine. He prefaced it by acknowledging that such spiritual practices had only become possible after his children were grown.[2] We appreciated the honesty. There are different seasons in life, and the parenting season is an intense one. So what does abiding in Christ look like when the baby was up half the night and the preschooler woke up way too early?

Ultimately, abiding in Christ is not about doing all the things but resting in who He made us to be. When we find our true identity in the One who created us, we are freed from the temptation to place our identity in outward appearances: how tidy our homes are, how well-behaved our children are, how long our quiet times lasted, or how much we accomplished.

We do not have to strive for, work for, negotiate or argue for, defend, or take credit for Christ's unconditional love for us. He is just as much at work in us when we're dancing in praise to Him as when we're dancing around toys on the floor. His faithfulness to us is just as steadfast when we read our Bible for an hour as when it sits in the car forgotten since last Sunday. His peace is available to us as surely when our children are tucked snugly in their beds and the house is quiet as it is when the chaos of screaming, crying, and tantrums is the soundtrack to our days.

How we wish we could help you grasp this indescribable freedom: Abiding in Christ is about His faithfulness and goodness, not about how hard we're holding on to Him. When we put Jesus at the center of our parenting and abide in Him, we radically surrender to our weakness so that we can depend wholly on His strength. The world tells us to defend ourselves by hiding, being ashamed of, and denying our flaws. Jesus invites us to welcome our weakness as a reminder to abide in Him.

In John 15, Jesus doesn't just talk about remaining in Him. He also talks about the Father pruning us so we will bear more fruit. This may sound like a negative thing, as pruning points to a stripping away. But the New Testament is full of language about abandoning or giving up the less valuable things of this world for the sake of following Jesus. Being in His Kingdom is the "pearl of great price" that is worth everything we might have in this world (Matthew 13:45-46, KJV).

Life in the Spirit

When the apostle Paul tried to describe the work of the Spirit in us, he used nine different words. He listed the fruit of the Spirit as "love, joy, peace, patience, kindness, goodness, faithfulness, gentleness, and self-control" (Galatians 5:22-23).

These attributes should characterize Christian parenting. We want to show our children love, share joy with them, and bring peace into our families. We try to deal patiently with our children's immaturity, be kind in our words and actions, and do what is right before God and our children. We are faithful to our children even when they are faithless, we are gentle in our attitudes and actions, and we choose to be in control of ourselves even when our children are out of control.

Looking at a list like the fruit of the Spirit can remind us of how many ways we fall short of these ideals. But Paul didn't write this passage to shame us when we're less than perfect. The fruit of the Spirit is not a to-do list on how to be better Christians. The fruit of the Spirit is the result of the work of God in us, which then leads us to live out these attributes. It's not an instant thing, either. We don't magically become more patient and peaceful the moment we start following Jesus. But the Holy Spirit within us does change our desires. Now we want to be patient, even though we are sometimes impatient.

Our desire to live in the Spirit changes our goal when dealing with our little ones. When they misbehave, embarrassing us or getting on our last nerve, our most important goal is not to stop the behavior or teach a lesson. Not that those are irrelevant; they're just not the most important objective. The ultimate goal is to live in the Spirit and show the fruit of the Spirit to our children. Whatever discipline, correction, connection, or boundary-enforcing that needs to happen in that moment, we can do it while displaying the fruit of the Spirit to our child.

What does the fruit of the Spirit look like as we relate to our children? Let's just take the first one, "love," and consider what it means. While the Bible describes love in many places, 1 Corinthians 13:4-5 includes a short, powerful description. These words reflect the biblical concept of love so vividly that they are often pulled from their original context—a description of the body of Christ—and personally applied to all relationships. This passage is often read at weddings to describe one's love for a spouse and can also be used to describe our love for our children. Let's consider all the different aspects of love mentioned and take a slightly snarky look at how our parenting often stacks up:

Patient—I'm trying, but this is really starting to try my
   patience.
Kind—I *kind* of speak and act with kindness toward my
   children.
Does not envy—I usually don't envy my kids, although I could
   use a little less responsibility and a lot more napping.
Not boastful—So long as bragging on my kids isn't a problem,
   I think I'm doing okay here.
Not arrogant—Is this implying that "Mother knows best" is
   not a great parenting plan?
Not rude—I'd like to draw a distinction here between being
   grumpy or snippy and being rude. My children can
   probably figure out the difference. Right?

Not self-seeking—Listen, I'm so busy seeing to everyone else's needs, I can't even remember what I actually want. So, not a problem.

Not irritable—I'm feeling personally attacked here.

Does not keep a record of wrongs—Look, I'm totally willing to forgive my children when they do wrong. But still, I'd like to hold it over them for a little bit, just to make sure they learn the lesson. Is that not okay?

We could go on through the rest of 1 Corinthians 13, but let's just say that when God sets the standard of love, He sets it really high. So high, in fact, that as parents we're not always going to meet it. This is why we need the work of the Spirit in us. It's also why we need grace. We know we need grace from God, but we also need it from our children. Thankfully, when they are young our children are quick to give it to us. Their grace covers a multitude of our failures. We want to cultivate that grace in our kids by giving grace to them as well. By God's grace, our never-perfected love for our children can become the exact love they need. But that starts with us and our choice to abide in Christ and then live a Spirit-filled, fruitful life with our children.

Posture of Peace

One way of cultivating and communicating peace to ourselves and to our children actually comes from the way we hold our bodies. Practice this posture of peace when responding to your child:

- Get below eye level.
- Open your arms; extend soft hands.
- Soften your jaw.
- Speak in a calm, steady voice.
- Use gentle touch.

Below eye level

Being on the same physical level, or lower, as your child helps them feel safer and more connected to you. Children have an immature threat detection response, so when they see you loom over them, they can perceive you as a menacing threat. Eye level or lower calms the amygdala, the part of the brain responsible for the fight-or-flight response, which disarms fear and threat perception.

Open arms and soft hands

Crossed and folded arms create a literal physical barrier between you and your child. When you keep your arms open and loose, it signals that you are open, receptive, welcoming, and approachable. Open arms naturally draw people to you and invite connection and comfort.

Soft jaw

Unclenching your jaw is more for your sake than for your child's. When you make the conscious effort to soften your jaw, neck, and shoulders, you release tension and relax your body. Though it's subtle, your child will pick up on the softness in your body and feel more safe and secure with you.

Calm, steady voice

When you are ready to speak, do it softly. If you're not able or ready to speak calmly and steadily, take a few slow, deep breaths while you think about what you will say. With as few words as possible, empathize with your child and communicate compassion. Your child's threat alarms will be disarmed, and they will feel safer.

Gentle touch

When a caregiver and a child are in close proximity to one another, the adult's calm central nervous system harmonizes with the child's, which helps guide them from a state of dysregulation and distress to a state of mutual, shared calm. This is known in neuroscience as co-regulation, and while it doesn't necessarily require physical touch, some children find it especially comforting to have a gentle hand placed on their shoulder or to be given a warm hug in the midst of their struggle. Note: Some children do not want to be touched when they are overstimulated. Unless there is an aspect of safety involved, honoring their bodily autonomy will serve to help them regulate faster than overriding their will with a gentle, albeit forced, touch.

The Dance of Chaos and Calm

In the sacred dance of life, amidst the whirlwinds of chaos and the tender melodies of everyday moments, we find ourselves seeking solace, yearning for a respite from the storms that occasionally batter our souls. It is in these very moments that we are beckoned to remember the divine posture that our Creator assumes toward us, His beloved children.

Imagine Almighty God, whose very voice formed the cosmos, bending His ear toward His creation, listening intently to the whispers of our hearts. His love is not distant or indifferent; it is the steady rhythm that beats beneath every heartbeat, the symphony that accompanies our every breath. Just as a good shepherd comes close to his sheep, our God leans close to us, nurturing a relationship in which He invites us to let go of fear and anxiety and cast them on Him because He cares for us (1 Peter 5:7).

And then, consider the Incarnation—Jesus Christ, the Word made flesh, who walked the very earth we tread. In the midst of chaos and tumult, He stepped down from the heavens and embraced the messiness of humanity. His very presence reminds us that in our moments of turmoil, we are not alone. He is the lighthouse that guides us through the tempest, the anchor that steadies our souls.

As parents journeying toward gentleness and peace, we can draw inspiration from God's posture toward us. Our pursuit of inner calm is not solely a personal quest; it is an echo of the divine call to attune ourselves to the rhythms of grace. Just as our bodies yearn for calm amidst chaos, our souls long for communion with the ultimate source of peace amidst life's clamor.

So, dear reader, as you navigate the intricate dance of parenting, remember that you are not left to weather the storm alone. Just as God bends His ear to hear your heart's whispers, be attuned to the whispers of your own soul. And just as Jesus embraced earthly chaos to bring heavenly peace, may you find solace in the midst of parenting's storms. In the delicate song of chaos and calm, may your heart find beautiful harmony, not discord, knowing that your fears and striving can cease, even when the storms do not.

Reflection Questions

1. What does abiding in Christ look like for you right now? Even if your margin of time is small, what's one way you can bring more awareness of Christ's life-giving, peacemaking presence in your life throughout the day?

2. As you consider the fruit of the Spirit, which one do you most hope to bring into your home, particularly as you engage with your children? What practical shift might you make to support that desire?

3. What specific activities or practices consistently help you reset and find peace in the midst of chaos? How can you

prioritize incorporating them into your routine? Who (if anyone) do you need to reach out to in order to help you prioritize these habits?

4. When it comes to spiritual disciplines, what practice do you find most helpful in cultivating inner peace and calm so that they can overflow into your family?

3

Cultivating Inner Peace

From my spot on our front porch swing, I could hear five-year-old Ezra and four-year-old Elijah giggling and squealing as they proudly showed off their newly acquired jump and flip tricks on the trampoline. Cries of "Mommy, watch me!" rang out as they tried to out-jump, out-tumble, and out-flip each other. As I watched, I was aware of how easily they could hurt each other without even trying. It wasn't hard to imagine them knocking heads or accidentally falling over each other and stepping on flailing limbs. Sure enough, they wound up bouncing toward the middle of the trampoline at exactly the same time, and one of their heads collided with the other's knee. Ezra, our oldest, jumped up and started dragging his younger brother to the edge of the trampoline. "You aren't playing safely, so you need to take a break and *get off*!" he yelled as he tried to push Elijah off the trampoline.

There's something about seeing one of your young children on the brink of getting hurt that activates a primal response of no-holds-barred protection. Before I knew it, I was screaming at Ezra. I practically flew to the trampoline, where I grabbed him by the arms and dragged him inside. "You are not being safe! You *cannot* try to push your brother off the trampoline! He could have fallen and broken something! We're going to take a break until you can play safely."

In that moment, I was beyond firm. I was yelling, pulling, and harshly reprimanding Ezra for overreacting to an accident.

You can see it, right? My words and my actions were nearly identical to Ezra's reaction to getting hurt. But I hadn't learned that from him—he'd learned it from me.

That incident on the trampoline will stick with me forever. In a way, it felt like an out-of-body experience, because my mama bear instinct took over, and even though I knew I was overreacting and being overly harsh, I couldn't stop myself. Later that night, I felt the gentle correction of the Holy Spirit. Even more than I wanted Ezra's behavior to change, I wanted *mine* to change.

A Whole-Person Approach to Inner Peace

From the trampoline incident and others like it, David and I realized how much our own words and actions were working against our desire for harmony within our home. Even before that, when our family began to navigate the messiness of postpartum anxiety after the birth of our second son, we quickly discovered the lack of resources for Christians that provide a holistic, whole-person approach to combating anxiety and cultivating peace. Christian resources tended to focus heavily on prayer, personal Bible study, and spiritual disciplines, while secular resources provided tremendously practical tools and coping skills but failed to address spiritual health and well-being.[1] We knew we needed both; anxiety and the rage that came with it touched every part of our lives—our relationships, the culture within our home, our parenting, and our spiritual disciplines.

Perhaps you can relate. That's why understanding what is going on in your body chemically, nutritionally, and hormonally—as well as spiritually—is another important part of your parenting journey. In the following pages you will find a holistic approach to cultivating inner peace in the midst of the chaos that raising children can bring. Of course, this is not intended to replace seeking professional diagnoses or care.[2] Rather, we hope to provide you with a new perspective on the anger, anxiety, and rage you may be experiencing in your everyday parenting moments. By understanding how your brain and body respond to stress, you can learn to work *with* your body in difficult moments.

A Biblical View of Science

Over the past fifty years, neuroscientists and psychologists have shed new light on how God designed the human brain to respond to threats and perceived danger. Once we realized that our reactions to the boys' misbehavior often flared instantaneously, we wondered what takeaways these disciplines might have for us. As Christians trying to parent with peace, however, we needed to consider a more fundamental question first: How much should Christians consider science and research, if at all?

One approach is to discount them altogether. Some people think that when God created the world, He left just the tiniest trace of His divine nature here. If we squint really hard, we might see a slight glimpse of Him. From this point of view, spending any effort examining God's creation is essentially useless. Some would have Christians look exclusively to the Bible because it's where God reveals Himself the most clearly. They believe that outside of the Bible there is really nothing true or wise to be found. But there's one slight problem with that view—the Bible itself contradicts it.

For example, Psalm 19 is one of many Scripture passages that talk about God's creation. Notice what it says:

The heavens declare the glory of God,
and the expanse proclaims the work of his hands.
Day after day they pour out speech;
night after night they communicate knowledge.

PSALM 19:1-2

The world that God created constantly tells us about Him. When we explore and examine creation, we should discover truth from God in it. The apostle Paul raises a similar point in Romans 1:

For [God's] invisible attributes, that is, his eternal power
and divine nature, have been clearly seen since the
creation of the world, being understood through what
he has made. As a result, people are without excuse.

VERSE 20

Paul then goes on to make an important observation: People can suppress, ignore, and reject the truth they see in the world. While God's truth is always evident in His creation, people can look at it without ever seeing it.[3] As Christians, that should give us pause before we uncritically accept or reject every interpretation of God's creation that people have put forward. After all, every human is impacted by sin, and there is always the possibility that we may be seeing the world inaccurately.

Some would argue that followers of Jesus have a better understanding of the world because we have the Bible and the Holy Spirit to help us. People without those advantages may have a mindset that colors their thinking and causes them to ignore or reject truth that should be clear to them. So we might conclude that even if we can learn truth from examining God's world, science—especially in the secular realm—is too compromised to be useful. But is that how the Bible treats all the observations of nonbelievers?

Truth is truth

Consider a man named Agur whose wise sayings are included in Proverbs 30. Clues in the text seem to indicate this otherwise unknown man was an Arabian wise man. He wasn't an Israelite, yet his wisdom was ultimately included in the book of Proverbs. Why does that matter? Because this reminds us that ancient Israel sometimes found truth and wisdom in their neighbors who weren't worshiping or following God. Agur wasn't an isolated incident, either.

Amenemope is a name you won't find anywhere in Scripture. But if you've read the Bible, you've read his words in Proverbs 22:17–24:22. Who was this unnamed writer? He was an Egyptian who lived many years before King Solomon and wrote a document called the Instruction of Amenemope. It contains thirty pieces of wisdom, which Proverbs 22:20 references: "Haven't I written for you thirty sayings about counsel and knowledge?" This seemingly random reference to thirty sayings—even though it's not connected to thirty proverbs—is like an ancient footnote pointing back to Amenemope.[4] But not all thirty of his sayings made it into Proverbs, and some of the ones that did have been heavily altered from their original form. Solomon, who compiled the book of Proverbs, didn't uncritically adopt Amenemope's words and declare them wisdom from God. He purposely filtered the sayings through his understanding of God, His character, His covenants, and His wisdom and freely accepted, rejected, or modified the wisdom originating from Egypt.

Here's the point—if ancient Israel could figure out how to discern potential truth or wisdom from idolatrous, pagan cultures, shouldn't we who have the Holy Spirit living within us be able to do the same today? The apostle Paul certainly seemed to think so!

In Acts 17, Paul was invited to speak to the philosophers of Athens. In his speech he quoted two well-known Greek poets, Epimenides and Aratus (see verse 28). You may have never heard of them, but they would have been very familiar to Paul's audience. Paul used lines from their writings to describe what God is like. Just one problem—these Greek poets didn't write about the God of Israel. They wrote about Zeus! Epimenides and Aratus got plenty of things wrong in their attempts to describe the divine. But they didn't get everything wrong. Paul took what was true and used it to preach Jesus.[5]

Truth is true, no matter who says it. Ultimately, all truth is God's truth. The clearest revelation of truth is found in God's Word. It is the ultimate authority, the lens through which all other human knowledge is examined, critiqued, and possibly found useful. But truth is also found beyond the pages of Scripture. By seeking it out, examining it, and accepting it, we find the very wisdom God's Word encourages us to pursue.

Scripture is sufficient

Some might argue that finding truth and wisdom outside the Bible undermines the authority of the Scripture. They might believe that looking for truth in neuroscience entails a rejection of the sufficiency of Scripture. Yet God revealed Himself in Scripture in order to bring humans into a renewed relationship with Him. It is entirely sufficient for every purpose God designed it to fulfill.

However, God didn't inspire the Bible to be a comprehensive guidebook to every aspect of life in God's creation.

Christians have long believed in the ultimate authority of Scripture while also acknowledging that it is not the solitary source of truth and doesn't speak to every single aspect of human life. The concepts of common grace (God's provision extends to all people, not only believers) and general revelation (some aspects of God can be known through nature) help us see that human experience, human reason, and human traditions can be powerful means of learning truth. All of these other sources coexist under a high view of Scripture as truthful, authoritative, and sufficient. While different Christian faith traditions have expressed these concepts in slightly different ways, the acceptance of other sources of wisdom under the authority of the Bible has been the historic Christian view. It has only been very recently that people have claimed that everything humans could possibly need to know for parenting or any other aspect of life can be found in the Bible. This kind of extreme "Bible-onlyism" cuts us off from all the wisdom God intends to be used to guide His children.

For example, the Bible speaks about cultivating fields, sowing seeds, reaping a harvest, and storing grain. But it's not a farmer's almanac. Through our human observations, systematized with science, we understand how to fertilize a field, rotate crops, create machines that allow us to plant and harvest with great precision, and store grain with minimal spoilage. Using modern farming methods is no more a denial of Scripture than using modern parenting methods. The key is that all claims to truth are tested against the wisdom found in God's authoritative Word.

We believe followers of Jesus can discover and use truth wherever it is found. We don't have to be scared or suspicious of the insights of neuroscience or psychology. Instead, we approach them with the full expectation that in them we will find a marvelous harmony between the revelation found in God's world and the one found in God's Word. Where such harmony is not evident, it is because we are misunderstanding either what we see in God's world or what we read in God's Word. Sometimes it might be a little bit of both! As Christians, we can get so focused on the few areas where this harmony is not immediately evident that we miss the overwhelming ways in which science reaffirms biblical teaching or provides more detailed insight into the application of biblical principles.[6]

Understanding the Stress Response Cycle

From our study of Scripture, then, we concluded that scientific discoveries do reveal truth about how God designed us. As we thought about the train table and trampoline incidents, we realized that understanding the stress response cycle helped explain our reactions to our young sons' altercations. This awareness was just one step on the journey of gaining inner peace. Knowing why we responded so quickly and forcefully didn't excuse our actions; rather, it provided a starting point in learning how we could moderate our responses in the future.

So, what is the stress response cycle? Imagine this: You're taking a walk at the park, and you see a big, menacing dog running toward you. Of course, your body and brain (particularly the amygdala, which acts as an alarm system) sense danger—and before you know it, you're running at breakneck speed. With heart pounding, breath racing, and body shaking, you hop in your car. Once you're safely inside, your breathing eventually slows and you start to feel relieved and grateful that you didn't get hurt. After a few more deep breaths you realize that you are completely safe. You survived, and you can move on with your day.

What you've experienced is known as a complete stress cycle, a biological process in the body that occurs as a response to any stress or crisis. It has a beginning, a middle, and importantly, an end. In order for your brain and body to feel safe and move forward after stress, you *have* to complete the stress response cycle.

This is where the issue arises: More than likely, your everyday stressors do not include defending yourself against an angry, rabid dog at the park! Instead, you're battling things like screaming children, smoke alarms, running late for appointments, work deadlines, relationship challenges, a crashing sound from another room, or having to clean up accidents and messes nonstop. The tricky thing is that these stressors probably aren't going away any time soon—and you aren't able to simply run from them. Yet if you don't provide your body with a way to complete the stress response cycle, you'll be stuck in perpetual survival mode.

If you've become easily provoked by your child's behavior, external factors like clutter and noise, and other triggering situations, it's empowering to truly understand what's happening. Put simply, this is your body trying to communicate with you: It doesn't feel safe. That's exactly how I (Amanda) felt when I realized that one of my sons was in danger on the trampoline.

The human brain is a remarkable thing. When it perceives a threat, the autonomic nervous system is activated and produces stress hormones, such as adrenaline and cortisol, that are necessary for survival. These hormones put you on high alert for any *additional* potential danger and also give your body energy to fight or flee the perceived threat. The problem is, the more these hormones are generated, the less ability you have to accurately differentiate between *perceived* threats (from everyday stressors) and *real* threats (life-threatening emergencies).[7] And thus the cycle continues, resulting in burnout, overwhelm, and hopelessness.

So what do we do? For many of us, our intuitive response is to try to eliminate as many stressors as we can. We try to manage our children's bad behavior so we don't get triggered. We clean up the clutter so we aren't overwhelmed by the chaos. We avoid social settings so we don't have to experience the anxiety that comes along with them. Unfortunately, avoidance is not a long-term healthy skill for nurturing inner peace or shalom—it simply helps us to continue surviving. We don't want to merely survive; we want to flourish. If eliminating stressors doesn't actually help us complete the stress response cycle, we must find ways to intentionally calm our brains' and bodies' response to the stress. So how can we do that?

Completing the Stress Response Cycle

Big body movement

It should come as no surprise that activities associated with survival instincts, such as running, crying, and screaming, are efficient ways to complete the stress cycle. I (David) naturally tend to use movement to handle stress. When things are challenging, you're likely to find me mowing the yard, working on the car, clearing a fence line, or chopping wood on our small farm. My favorite way to get stress out is to sweat it out.

Of course, it's not always possible to do hard, grungy work while simultaneously keeping a toddler safe or helping siblings navigate an argument over whose turn it is to use the red crayon. But there are a variety of activities that will trigger the completion of a stress response cycle and return your brain and body to a state of peace and calm. That will then reengage the rational, thinking parts of your brain so you can problem-solve and regulate your impulses. For Amanda and me, incorporating big body movement in everyday life looks like blocking out daily trampoline time for our boys (because—spoiler alert—kids have stress response cycles as well!) and hiking in our nearby woods when the weather permits.

Psychiatrist James Gordon details how big movement is healing for the body and mind, explaining that many cultures have been shaking, dancing, and stomping out their tensions for most of human history: "All our ancestors . . . shouted and danced and whirled and jumped up and down. When something terrible had happened or was about to happen, they moved their bodies and let go of their tensions and expressed their feelings."[8]

These ancient practices now have modern science to explain their effectiveness. Brisk physical activity and big body movement help your brain complete a stress response cycle by using up (therefore minimizing the presence of) adrenaline and cortisol, two of the primary stress hormones. Activities like dancing, jumping rope or doing jumping jacks, big belly laughing, strong hugging, and shaking your body are all ways to help regulate your mental and physical state.

Mindful breathing and meditation

In Genesis 2, we read that God breathed life into dust to animate the crowning achievement of His creation: humankind. It makes sense then that breathing has a powerful effect on the human body.

I (Amanda) first learned about mindful breathing in counseling for my postpartum anxiety. My counselor taught me four-square breathing, a technique that involves inhaling through your nose to a count of four, holding your breath for a four count, exhaling through your mouth at the same or slower pace, and holding your lungs empty to the count of four before inhaling and beginning the cycle again. Four-square breathing is just one mindful breathing technique that can calm the body and regulate the parts of the brain that are responsible for completing the stress response. I still use four-square breathing when I feel overwhelmed and need to recenter myself, but I also use it early in the morning when I first wake up so that I intentionally start my day regulated and calm.

By refocusing the mind, meditation also helps complete the stress response cycle. When I meditate, I like to focus my attention on Scriptures that speak to the character and nature of God. I often need reminding of God's compassion, long-suffering, faithfulness, and provision for His people in their most desolate days.

Though Scripture invites us to practice centering our thoughts on God, His statutes, and His goodness, Christians often shy away from meditation because it seems rooted in Eastern mysticism. Yet for most of Christian history, meditation and contemplation have been viewed as important spiritual disciplines that are crucial to the flourishing of God's people. From ancient church fathers and medieval mystics to Reformers like John Calvin and influential American theologians like Jonathan Edwards and Francis Asbury, meditation and contemplation have been encouraged and practiced widely among Christians.[9]

Again, when we look to science, we see that God's created work complements and brings clarity to His written Word. A 2015 study found that practicing consistent mindfulness and meditation can dampen the amygdala's activity, effectively reducing reactivity to common stressors and contributing to a quicker recovery from stress.[10] While other religions and practitioners may teach focusing on one mantra or chant, or even emptying the mind, we as Christians know that when we empty ourselves before the cross of Jesus and focus on Him, He fills us, transforms our minds, and creates a new heart within us, making us to be more like Him.

Social connections

I (Amanda) remember when my counselor asked me how much time I was spending connecting with my close friends. I laughed out loud and leaned back on the couch, pulling a pillow onto my lap. "I do playdates sometimes, but it's hard to connect because we are all watching our babies," I said.

After a long discussion and the creation of an action plan, I left that counseling session with instructions to spend at least two hours over the next two weeks connecting with my friends—without our children along for the ride. That meant David would have to figure out how to do something we'd been carefully avoiding since our second son was born—put a baby and a toddler to bed while parenting solo. But my making social connections mattered to him. So after a few foibles and aborted bedtimes, he figured it out.

Social connections play an important role in minimizing our stress responses. Of course they do! We are made in God's image and wired to be in a community of deep connection. Laughter, affection, and the happiness and bonding hormones that flow in safe social situations play a key role in maintaining emotional and mental wellness. Parents of young children in particular can find it difficult to prioritize social time with friends, and postpartum anxiety and depression add an additional barrier to creating rhythms of community connection. I say this gently, and with so much compassion: Work through the fear of leaving your little ones with another (sometimes nonparental) caregiver rather than avoiding it. The benefits are worth it, and the more you do it, the more your brain will recognize that it is safe to do so.

Rest

Going back to Genesis 2, we remember that on the seventh day, God rested. Rest is a recurring and important theme throughout Scripture. From Israel's Sabbath observance to the eternal rest described in Hebrews 4, rest is a divine gift that runs throughout the entirety of God's story. Following that thread would be a book in itself, and while we can't touch on every aspect here, it is important to note that rest is a key part of human flourishing, including thriving as parents.[11]

We found out we were pregnant with Elijah when Ezra was just nine months old. That surprise second pregnancy forced us to face head-on the reality of our God-given need for rest. We enrolled

Ezra in a Mother's Day Out program at a local church and joked that we paid sweet church ladies to babysit Ezra just so Amanda could sleep two days a week.

Physical rest is necessary for us to recover from the stress response cycle. Truly, it is no wonder that parents of young children feel overwhelmed and overstressed! And while physical rest is vitally important, the idea of whole-person rest comes home to our parenting in at least a couple of ways. A lot of the ideas in this book won't make sense to you if you think you must work hard to earn God's approval rather than resting in the finished work of Christ. Parenting is exhausting. If there is one thing that is truly universal to parents, it's the need to unwind.

Yet many parents struggle with prioritizing rest and creating rhythms and systems in their homes that allow for as much rest as is needed. We must remember that God does not measure people by their productivity or appearance. Rather, it is our culture that suggests that every house needs to be spotless, every baby needs to be Instagram ready, every mother needs perfect hair, and every father needs to climb the ladder of success. That pressure we feel to do more and be more? It doesn't come from God. He invites us to rest. More than that, He designed us to need rest, so there's no shame in needing it.

Be Responsive and Proactive

When we understand the body's neurological and physical response to stressors, we are empowered to be both *responsive* in difficult moments as well as *proactive* throughout the day to establish inner peace in our bodies, souls, and minds. The authors of *Burnout: The Secret to Unlocking the Stress Cycle* recommend practicing one or more stress-cycle-completing activities (such as the ones in the sidebar) for twenty to sixty minutes most days of the week.[12]

EIGHT WAYS TO COMPLETE A STRESS CYCLE (EVEN WITH LITTLE KIDS!)

1. Schedule a dance-off with your little ones before supper.
2. Practice mindful breathing during kids' nap time.
3. Watch comedy that makes you belly laugh.
4. Go for a run, jog, or swim.
5. Paint and hide rocks with your children.
6. Find art lessons online that you can do with your child.
7. Go out with friends while your spouse enjoys time with the kids.
8. Jump on a trampoline with your kiddos.

Cultivating inner calm during the mayhem and pandemonium of parenting takes remarkable strength. In the midst of mounting pressure, it's easy to lose control of our emotions and act impulsively. These are signs that our bodies and minds have become dysregulated, or quite literally have lost the ability to moderate emotions and impulses. As you go through your day, check in on your breathing and how you are holding stress in your body; this will help alert you to the early signs of being dysregulated and prompt you to take a few minutes to nurture and care for your needs.

Some early signs of dysregulation include:

- difficulty focusing
- tightening of the neck, shoulders, or lower back
- shallow breathing
- feeling snappy and overly fidgety
- checking out
- clenching of the hands or jaw
- sensitivity to touch or noise

We'll go into more detail about dysregulation in chapter 7, but for now, when you notice these signs in yourself (or your children!), we encourage you to pause and take a few minutes to regulate. It's worth it. You can use the ideas in this chapter, or for more ideas, check out the resources on our website about regulating your nervous system.[13] What works for one person may not work for you. Instead of getting discouraged, keep listening to what your body is telling you. Remember, we were made for peace.

Reflection Questions

1. How would you describe your current level of inner peace? What aspects of your life contribute positively or negatively to this state?

2. How do you typically respond to your own emotions, especially the difficult ones? How might your children be learning from your example?

3. Consider a time when you reacted with frustration or impatience toward your child's behavior. How might the situation have unfolded differently if you'd responded calmly? What steps can you take to cultivate patient responses in the future?

4. What specific techniques might you adopt to enhance your physical calmness during high-stress parenting moments? How might these practices positively impact your children's emotional development?

4

Playing the Long Game

"There's a reason God designed parenting to start with a cute, cuddly little baby!" I (David) said under my breath a few minutes after our eleven-year-old foster son slammed—and I mean *slammed*—his bedroom door. It was the kind of slam that shook the walls, rattled the windows, and knocked an *entire shelf* off the wall—a desperate attempt to make sure we knew just how angry he was.

When we welcomed three foster children into our home late one August afternoon, we were full of good intentions and hopeful expectations. We were going to show these not-yet-men but no-longer-children so much love and speak enough life over them to make up for all the loss they'd experienced in their short lives. Soon after they arrived, we loaded everyone into our car and went out for pizza, and as we sat around the table laughing, silently shocked at just how much they could eat in one sitting, we were sure this was going to be good. We knew God had called us to foster these three boys, whom we affectionately referred to as Cowboy, Wrangler, and Red on social media to protect their identities and honor their stories, which aren't really ours to tell.

The first few weeks were a weird combination of really hard and really fulfilling. The boys settled into their rooms (which were fully furnished and decorated because our family and friends came alongside us and provided everything we could want or need to make our home welcoming and comfortable for these three kids with almost nothing to their names), and we found reliable routines that set us up for pleasant-ish days. As pleasant as they could be, under the circumstances.

That was the honeymoon phase.

A few weeks later we faced daily challenges and struggles that we were painfully ill-equipped to handle. By the time Christmas came and went, one of the boys had been suspended from riding the school bus, and another was rapidly heading toward having a chat with authorities about some could-be-criminal choices he'd made while at school.

At home, it felt like we were stuck in a never-ending cycle: We'd impose a consequence, they'd come back with even *worse* behavior, resulting in an even *worse* consequence that did little to correct or de-escalate the situation . . . we were exhausted. Legally, foster parents are limited in how they can discipline bad behavior, and our lack of parenting experience made us feel even more helpless. The night the door was ferociously slammed, we did the only thing we knew to do at the time: We took the door off its hinges as punishment for slamming it in our faces.

At the time it seemed like the best thing to do. It was a logical consequence, and it came with the seemingly added benefit of impacting his brothers since they shared a room. They had to learn that their actions had consequences and affected others, right? These boys needed to learn how to be men!

We kept the door off for a week. For seven days I went to bed every night wondering if this was a reasonable consequence. It wasn't really teaching the eleven-year-old (or his brothers) anything. Not how to handle his anger when he was on the verge of being overcome by it. Not how to communicate effectively so that he could be heard and understood even in his frustration or distress. It wasn't even really teaching him to value our home or his relationships. In fact, it mostly just fostered bitterness and more strife in our home.

We were giving those boys everything we had, yet I couldn't shake the thought that they deserved better.

Moving Away from Fear

Later, when we were in the throes of toddlerhood with our biological children and finally moving toward a new parenting perspective, we learned why we felt so trapped and exhausted in the "consequence cycle" with our foster boys: Negative, fear-based consequences do nothing to teach positive, honor-based behavior. We came by our instincts honestly; fear-based parenting techniques are ubiquitous in modern Western culture. From threatening to give a spanking to taking away privileges, the general idea that fear of negative consequences will motivate children to comply with rules and limits is nearly universal. And it overflows into day cares and classrooms. From our response to the earliest sign of defiance in a tiny toddler to the thick section on discipline included in the student handbook we give to college students, our world is set up to have children controlled, manipulated, and managed primarily through fear.

At first, even with our biological children, our home was no different. Threats, warnings, and negative consequences were as normal to us as kissing boo-boos and telling bedtime stories. Even after we began parenting with peace and purpose, it took several years for us to fully embrace a nonpunitive parenting approach that allowed us to guide our children with love, gentle firmness, inner peace, and Spirit-led patience. We first had to understand *what* "fear-based" really means and *why* it doesn't work in the long-term. Then we set out on the yearslong task of unlearning the impulse to use fear to control our children. And with that, we had to unlearn the fear of how our kids might turn out if we didn't use fear-based tactics.

But neuroscience and Scripture are clear: Fear is a powerful motivator, but love is more powerful still.

Underneath It All

Just as understanding what is going on in our bodies chemically, nutritionally, hormonally, and spiritually is an important part of our parenting journeys, understanding these components in our children's bodies is of equal importance. Similar to our own, children's brains are not wired to differentiate well between a perceived threat and a real threat. Further, their lack of knowledge and experience makes them even less adept at recognizing this distinction. This means when we use a threat or negative consequence to control our children's behavior, their brains perceive a threat and elicit a *real* stress response accordingly. Remember the angry dog from chapter 3? Imagine it's going after your kid—only in this case, the angry dog is you.

The brain's alert detection sequence takes less than two-hundredths of a second, which is significantly faster than a cognitive thought process.[1] What this means in practicality is that your child's brain will engage a fear response before it has time to consider if the threat is real or how serious the threat is. When we use punishment and negative consequences to discourage unwanted behavior, it signals threat detection alarms in the brain. Many parents are already familiar with what this looks like when a fight response is activated in their child: pushing back, power struggles, escalating emotions, and doing everything in their power to control what they can.

But the other three survival instincts are less easily recognized, and that's because those responses look an awful lot like the compliance we're hoping for:

- Flight response:
  - stops unwanted behavior
  - runs away
  - may hide
  - avoids parent, sibling, or situation that caused the stress response

- Freeze response:
  - stops unwanted behavior
  - becomes quiet
  - looks very "compliant"
  - stops or slows down body

- Fawn response:
  - stops unwanted behavior
  - tries to appease adult
  - seeks to gain parental approval and affection

You can see how this presents a problem for parents, right? Three out of four fear responses give the illusion of well-behaved, obedient, and compliant kids! We suspect this is one reason why fear-based discipline is alluring and so ubiquitous: It looks like it works! But in reality, the child's reaction is almost certainly a stress response triggered by the brain to protect the child from a perceived threat.

That's the hard truth we as Christian parents must confront: When we get a child to obey, but they're doing it in order to stay safe or feel loved by their parent, it's not character formation; it is not creating good habits; it is not Jesus-centered discipleship or heart change. It is survival.

Short-Term Success, Long-Term Effects

As long as the unwanted behavior stops, what's the problem? It's a valid question.

I (Amanda) remember an instance when I put Ezra in the naughty chair when he was newly two. It was not over a major incident; he simply wasn't obeying me when I told him it was time to get dressed.

Intuitively, we had put the chair in a public space rather than making Ezra sit alone in his room. This decision was based on what we know of God more than on any trending parenting advice at the time. After all, we are told over and over again in Scripture that God "will never leave you nor forsake you" (Deuteronomy 31:6, NIV), that we cannot escape the presence of God (Psalm 139:7-10), and that nothing can separate us from the love of God (Romans 8:35-39).

I remember watching Ezra sit there and thinking to myself, *How is this accomplishing anything? He's still not getting dressed! He's not learning to get dressed. And he's not getting any closer to obedience.*

As we continued questioning, studying, and praying for wisdom, we learned another key fact about how our brains are designed. When the brain triggers a stress response, the parts of the brain primarily responsible for learning are diminished, or worse, shut down completely. When a fear response is activated, we operate purely from survival. This may not seem all that important, but it proves to be a fundamental pillar of parenting: If the learning centers of the brain aren't functioning optimally (or worse, aren't operating at all), a child quite literally *can't* learn the lesson their parents and teachers want them to learn.[2]

This creates a terrible cycle that is, in many ways, counterproductive to our long-term parenting goals. If a child is dysregulated or feeling threatened, further consequences and punishments only trigger them and—you guessed it—cause more negative behavior. Which leads to more consequences, which leads to more negative behavior . . .

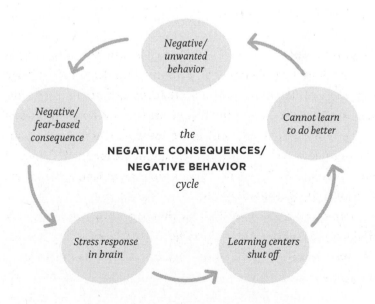

Negative/ unwanted behavior

Negative/ fear-based consequence

Cannot learn to do better

the
NEGATIVE CONSEQUENCES/ NEGATIVE BEHAVIOR
cycle

Stress response in brain

Learning centers shut off

On and on the cycle goes. There are only two ways to stop it:

1. The child eventually gives up (a freeze or fawn response) and begins to comply and withdraw.
2. We as parents interrupt the cycle by minimizing and moving away from negative and fear-based consequences and harnessing the power of connection, trust, and grace-based accountability instead.

When we actively choose not to rely on fear-based consequences, we not only bring more trust and health to our family, but we also help create a new cycle of learning in our children's brains.

Yes, it may take longer to correct the unwanted behavior, and we know that can be frustrating! But that's because learning takes time, and trust is something that must be cultivated throughout the learning process.

Consider another example: Recently, our boys were fighting over a new dinosaur toy. And I mean, a *brand-new* toy. It had been in our possession for less than twenty-four hours. These days our kiddos do fairly well at solving problems together. They've had many years of practicing collaboration, and they both are developing their still-somewhat-immature moral compasses. This time, however, with a shiny new toy on the line, they were resorting to might makes right. I (Amanda) heard their squabble elevate to an outright fighting match. By the time I entered the arena—er, living room—Elijah was hoisting a toy light saber and was ready to strike. Before he could fully give in to the dark side, I stooped down close to him and took hold of the light saber to ensure immediate safety.

It took a while (as both of our boys felt deeply that they should be able to play with the new toy first and longest), but I was able to work through problem-solving and repairing the relationship between the two of them. When a solution had been found, I asked Elijah if he was able to play with the light saber safely.

"I think I'm able to *try*," he said honestly.

"All right, then! Show me what it looks like to play with it safely."

And with a few swipes through the air and his very own sound effects, Elijah was off on an adventure while he waited for a turn with the new toy.

A few hours later Ezra and I debriefed the incident. I could tell he had questions, and I invited him to ask them.

THE FEAR OF THE LORD

Anytime we talk about fear and parenting, we often get asked about the "fear of the Lord." That's a good question; after all, Proverbs 1:7 says, "The fear of the LORD is the beginning of knowledge."

Typically there are a couple of different responses to the fear of the Lord. Some people will say, "Fearing God is good; that's why I use fear in my parenting." Others will say, "Fear is a bad parenting strategy, so I will not teach my children to be scared of God." Both of these views misunderstand the fear of the Lord. It's not about being anxious before the Lord as if we are simpering servants hoping to avoid our master's anger. Nor is it about being scared because God is some kind of erratic, abusive father.

Instead, the fear of the Lord is about discovering who He truly is—that He is not just the Creator and Ruler of all things, but a Father who gave His own Son for us to take away our sins. He is a Son who reconciles us to Himself and is unashamed to call us, who are the children of God, His brothers and sisters (Hebrews 2:11-12). The fear of the Lord calls us to wake from our foolish stupor and begin to live as His children. The fear of the Lord is reverence, awe, and respect, but it's also a recognition of who we are in relation to Him.[3]

We can lead our children to the fear of the Lord, but we will never do it by making them fear us. The fear of man never leads to the fear of the Lord. This is why we have persistently advocated against using fear in parenting. It doesn't accomplish our disciplinary goals or our spiritual goals, and it carries with it significant consequences for our children and our relationships with them.

"I really thought you should have taken the light saber away," he said tentatively.

"Oh yeah? How come?"

He shifted in his seat and shrugged his shoulders. "I dunno. It just seemed like it should be put away."

One thing I try really hard not to do is make assumptions about what my kids are thinking. Okay, I still make assumptions, but I do my best to remain deeply curious, especially when we're having conversations about behavior and consequences.

"Do you think putting it away would have been a good consequence for someone almost getting hurt?" I asked.

He shrugged his shoulders again. Bless the shoulder shrug.

"I dunno. It wouldn't have helped us learn how to solve a problem or how to use the toy the right way. I know that."

Our boys are older, so we tend to be pretty open about our parenting perspective; Ezra understands that, in general, the goal of consequences is restoration and equipping for next time. (See chapter 9 for more on these concepts.) I stayed quiet to see if he would say anything else. Sure enough, he continued. "I guess putting it away wouldn't have really taught us anything. It probably would have made Elijah mad, too, which would have made things worse, actually."

I will freely admit, my mama heart was leaping with joy—my thoughtful, intuitive little guy got it. It was hard in the moment of conflict to resist the urge to intervene, but if I had put the light saber away, what would they have learned? That mom puts away toys we use for weapons. Putting away the toy might make sense in the moment (and with younger children, and in more dangerous situations, putting away a toy may in fact be helpful in holding limits and keeping children safe), but it would fail to teach them what they needed to learn right then and there: impulse control, problem-solving skills, empathy, kindness, and peacemaking. Putting the toy away wouldn't teach any of those things, and it would work against most of them!

That's the thing about punishments and fear-based control: They usually require escalating consequences to keep the child in check. It's the fuel for the cycle, and it makes for a dizzying, miserable ride. By slowing down and intentionally choosing the path of trust and love, both parent and child learn something important. And the best part is, that only deepens the connection between them.

LONG-TERM CONSEQUENCES OF FEAR

Child-development experts have been studying the effects of fear-based parenting for decades, and the research consistently reveals negative outcomes in the areas of mental health, interpersonal relationships, and job performance. (Interestingly, negative consequences in the workplace also result in poorer job performance. People of all ages are naturally resistant to negative and fear-based consequences.[4])

Fear-based parenting approaches have been linked to:

- depression
- anxiety
- alcohol abuse
- social anxiety (agoraphobia)
- eating disorders
- teenage rebellion
- fractured parent-child relationship later in life[5]

These studies aren't all that surprising when we think about how we as adults would respond to the same levels of control our children face each day.

Our care and nurturing of children in their early years impacts their future mental health. Of course, this isn't the only influence; there are countless factors, many of which are beyond our control, that influence flourishing in adulthood. But the data is clear that how we show up as parents when our children are young greatly affects them later in life.

The Good, Good Father

Jesus understood the power of love better than any person before or after Him. And when we consider His teaching in the parable of the good, good father (Luke 15:11-32), we see how transformative it can be. After all, Jesus was telling this parable to religious leaders who in their pride thought Jesus shouldn't be spending time with imperfect people.

When most of us read the story of this good father, we focus on his wayward son or the self-righteous older brother who shows up later. Many of us can identify with the Prodigal Son: He messes up his entire life by acting with incredible selfishness and is in obvious need of forgiveness. Others can relate to the older brother, the dutiful "good" person who would like a little bit of credit for not being "that bad." From the former we learn the power of redemption; from the latter, we learn the dangers of pride.

Yet, for us, it's the father whose behavior is truly bonkers. He is the central person in the story—and his behavior holds a key insight for us as parents today.[6]

When the Prodigal Son asks for his inheritance, his demand is about more than money. It's rooted in a desire to end relationships and destroy the family. He wants nothing to do with his father. He wants his father dead. But since that hasn't happened yet, he wants his inheritance. Once he gets the money, he plans to go "no contact" (severing all relationship and communication) with his family.

In a shockingly bold move that outright breaks the fifth commandment, this son has refused to honor his father. He has brought him shame. What would you do if someday this was how your adult child treated you? You probably wouldn't be inclined to give them a lot of money—a totally valid response! In the culture of the time, the father would have been expected to react to his son's brazen demand very negatively. The father doesn't do any of that. He doesn't even threaten it. He never uses fear or shame to bring back his wayward son; nor does he express any interest in the capital punishment that could be given to rebellious sons (Deuteronomy 21:18-21).

Instead, the father heaps shame onto himself in the eyes of the surrounding community. He doesn't reject his son's shame; he takes it on himself. The gracious father chooses to give his son what he demands. He gives away some of his wealth. What does this cost the father? We don't know, but it seems the father is a wealthy farmer. That means his assets aren't just sitting in the bank. The things he owns are what he uses to make money. Selling off land or flocks casts a long shadow into the future, as all the income they could produce in the coming years will not happen. What the father gives to the son is not just wasted by the son's profligate ways, but it also destroys all the benefits that could have accrued to the family from them. Yet the father gives them away.

By this point, most of us are probably thinking that this story offers terrible parenting advice. The father is letting his son get away with absolutely horrible behavior! He not only fails to correct the boy, but he also indulges him by giving him what he asked for! This seems like the complete and total opposite of every scrap of parenting advice we've ever received.

But that's the point, isn't it? The father in this story does what no human father would dream of doing; he is endlessly gracious. The father is God Himself. The point of the parable for us as parents is not that we should give our children everything they ever ask for and hope for the best. The point is that the God we are teaching our children about is a God of endless grace.

We won't introduce them to that God by using fear and punishment to try to form their character, forcing them into compliance through threats and strong voices. In doing so, our actions will only contradict our words. Rather, children learn about a God of grace through our own graciousness. We can train, discipline, and mold our children while maintaining a posture of peace and grace toward them. Our human grace may be imperfect and far more limited than the grace God offers, but it still molds young hearts far better than fear ever can.

The Love of a Father

In chapter 9, we'll talk more about the father's response when his wayward son returns. But the story of the good, good father isn't just the story of a ne'er-do-well son. It's the story of a father. And he has two sons. The older son is the son everyone wants to have. He's compliant and dutiful. He puts the needs of his family ahead of his desires. He's the polar opposite of his lousy little brother. He's the kind of son that for millennia has made parents swell with pride and say things like, "I didn't do everything right, but look at how my son turned out. He sure has made me proud."

When the older son appears in the story, he is frustrated and angry. He comes home after a long day of work, the most recent of many, many long days working on the family farm. He hears the sounds of an unscheduled party. This is unexpected, so he asks one of the servants what is going on. After learning that the party is for his selfish, greedy, shameful little brother, he refuses to participate. He has no grace for his brother, who had long ago proven he had no love for his family.

What does the father do? The same thing he did earlier in the day with his younger son. He goes to his older son. He doesn't demand that the son come in and join the party. Instead, he leaves the celebration to seek out his son. When the father reaches him, the older son is full of fury. Pride and vanity burst forth in a string of insults aimed at the father. He's built his identity around being the "good son," and now he demands to know why the father doesn't recognize his evident superiority with similar lavish celebrations.

The father doesn't respond with anger or demands. He has grace for his son's anger and bitterness. He meets his self-righteousness with compassion. But he does speak with a sharp clarity, emphasizing that his older son is as far from him as the younger son once was. The older son is just as loved as his brother, but he can't see it because he's still trying to earn his father's love.

Here's the amazing thing about this father's love. Not only can his sons not lose it by outrageous, shameful actions, but also they cannot earn it by good, faithful actions. The father loves his sons, no matter who they are or what they've done.

Too often, our habits imply to our children that they must earn our love. We make our love more pronounced if they do what we want, if they listen and comply. (And if we use fear-based techniques, this disparity becomes even more obvious.) This is the sister of parenting with fear—making our children feel as if they must earn our love. Not only can we use fear as a weapon to keep our children from certain actions, but we can also use our love as an inducement to do the things we want them to do.

If we want to introduce our children to the love of God and show them His love, we must look to the example the father in the parable shows us—unearned, unending love. This is biblical fatherhood. This is fathering to be the image of God to our children. Yes, we'll always be an imperfect mirror of God's love to our children, but we can be a mirror nonetheless.

The Harvest of Love

I (Amanda) was listening to my boys play one morning when I overheard a conversation between them that left me picking my jaw up off the floor. Ezra said in his most gentle toddler voice, "You're in my space, Elijah. Can you play somewhere else?" And Elijah, who was barely two at the time, said, "Okay!" and happily moved around to the other side of their train table. This was the moment we had been practicing for months! *Gentle parenting actually works!*

Up until that moment I still had some doubts. Oh, I was committed to not using fear-based parenting strategies to manage behavior. But I was more hopeful than confident that it would "work." When we started out on a new parenting journey as peacemakers, it seemed like we were constantly asking ourselves, *Is this really working?* or *Am I disciplining enough?* or *Why aren't they learning this faster?* We were overly familiar with short-term compliance and underinformed on child development, so replacing behavior modification with long-term problem-solving skills often felt ineffective. Add to that the way society rewards and applauds parents for keeping their children quiet, still, and obedient (regardless of whether it is developmentally appropriate), and still frowns upon parents whose children are less than compliant and convenient, and we frequently wondered whether we were on the right track.

That January morning proved to be a turning point for me. Listening in on our kids' problem-solving abilities after practicing with them so many times was just a tiny glimpse into how cultivating peace could play out. And to be fair, it also proved to be a rare occurrence for several years, as our two- and three-year-olds continued to navigate many sibling dynamics with healthy doses of immaturity!

But witnessing that small peacemaking scene between my boys felt like an embodiment of a verse in 1 John:

> There is no fear in love; instead, perfect love drives out fear, because fear involves punishment. So the one who fears is not complete in love.
>
> 1 JOHN 4:18

The work we had been doing with our children to intentionally parent with peace and purpose hadn't been easy (and it still isn't!). Fear may seem like a shortcut to peace because love takes a lot longer to cultivate. But when we get to reap that harvest of love and trust—there's nothing better.

Reflection Questions

1. Recall a situation in which fear influenced your parenting decision, perhaps even leading you to punish your child harshly. How did this approach affect your child's response and overall well-being? Reflect on how the principle of parenting with unconditional love might have altered the outcome.

2. Consider a recent instance when your child exhibited behaviors resembling obedience or compliance. Could these behaviors have been linked to survival instincts like flight, freeze, or fawn? How might understanding this reshape your approach to discipline?

3. The parable of the good, good Father illustrates a father's choice to show unmerited favor and affection. How does this resonate with your own parenting journey? Can you identify moments when extending grace and trust yielded positive results that punishment might not have achieved?

4. Think about your ultimate parenting goals and the legacy you want to leave for your children. How does adopting a peace-focused, trust-centered approach align with these aspirations? How might this approach contribute to a more fulfilling and harmonious family dynamic over time?

PART 2

Parenting with Peace and Purpose

Created for Connection

I (Amanda) remember when our older son was born.

After five years of infertility, countless tests and treatments, and an early pregnancy loss eleven months prior, we were eager to welcome our first child into our arms. Like most new mamas, I had hopes and dreams of a meaningful and trauma-free birth experience. We had planned a peaceful, unmedicated, out-of-hospital birth with a wonderful midwifery team and birth doula. Our birth center was a hundred-year-old Victorian mansion nestled in the historic medical district of a nearby city. Because our journey to pregnancy had been so long and came with many deeply felt losses, this pregnancy was redemptive in many ways. My birth experience, too, had been set up to be peaceful, picturesque, and healing.

I noticed moderately strong contractions while David and I were on a (very slow) evening walk three days before my guess date.

My birthing classes had convinced me that first-time moms usually go into natural labor around forty-one weeks, so we were not anticipating our baby's birthday coming anytime soon. We hadn't even finished packing a birth bag! But after those few moderate contractions on our walk, we waddled home and started tracking the waves. It was time.

We arrived in the quiet, calm, and welcoming birthing room, and our midwifery team let us know that I was indeed in active labor. All of the work and preparation I had done with my doula seemed to be paying off—I felt confident, in control, and fully present. Ezra was coming, they told me, and he was coming soon.

Unfortunately, the rest of the birth didn't go as planned. Ezra shifted in my womb to a breech position. Our birth team monitored Ezra's heart rate closely and attempted to turn him, but to no avail. With our history of infertility and loss, we were not willing to take any additional risks, and we knew the best call was to transfer to the hospital, where I would have an emergency C-section.

Reflecting back, the details are still fuzzy to me. I remember doing everything in my power not to push and to stay calm as I prepared to leave the birthing center. Now in the last stage of labor, with my doula and midwife doing their best to keep me covered, I walked down the stairs, out the door, and down the walkway to the waiting ambulance. For a long time, that journey was my proudest moment during my son's birth. In spite of our plan going so awry, I was strong, confident, and in control of my body.

It wasn't until I was rolled into the operating room and David *had* to let go of my hands that I finally felt the anxiety of the moment. I was alone. I was freezing cold yet sweating uncontrollably, and the lights were beyond bright—this was never how I had imagined it would go. The anesthesiologist counted me down from three, and before I could reach two, everything went black.

A few minutes later, Ezra entered the world.

A little over an hour later, I woke to soft voices, but I couldn't really determine what they were saying. "I need a drink," I croaked. Everything in me—mind, body, and soul—hurt.

I wish I could tell you that I remember meeting Ezra, or what I said or how I felt when I laid eyes on my miracle rainbow baby for the first time. I wish I could tell you that I remember watching David with the biggest smile on his face, joy emanating from every fiber of his being, as he held this not-so-tiny newborn in his arms. But I can't.

For months I had envisioned and prayed over the moment I would meet my long-awaited son and gaze upon his squishy pink face for the first time. But Ezra's first moments on earth were in a sterile operating room completely devoid of his parents' adoring gazes and soothing words. Not only had our carefully prayed-over and hoped-for plan gone awry, but I was not even conscious when my beautiful newborn took his first breaths! I wasn't the first to hold him and nurture him. The first voices he heard weren't his mama and daddy joyfully cooing over him. How would this affect him? Would we still experience that all-consuming maternal-infant bond all the baby books talked about? While I knew that the sudden change in our birth plan was outside my control, I couldn't shake the nagging question of whether I was a good mom or had somehow managed to mess it all up already.

Trust Begins with Attachment

While extreme and rooted in anxiety, my concerns weren't completely unfounded. We have learned more about the human brain and how it works in the last twenty-five years than in all of past human history combined, thanks to advancing discoveries in the fields of psychology and neurology. Technology has enabled us to peer further inside ourselves than ever before. We've discovered

WHAT IS SECURE ATTACHMENT?

Attachment theory, developed by psychologist John Bowlby, offers profound insights into the emotional bonds that shape human relationships, particularly between parents and children. Attachment refers to the deep and enduring emotional connection established between infants and their primary caregivers, typically their parents.

Securely attached children tend to exhibit greater emotional resilience, self-esteem, and social competence as they grow. They possess a solid foundation from which to explore the world, knowing their caregivers are dependable sources of support. This security enables them to develop healthy relationships, regulate emotions effectively, and confidently navigate life's challenges.

that each and every one of us has a neurological and biological need for deep connection, secure attachment, felt safety, and trust. In fact, these things are necessary for humans to truly flourish.

At the heart of parenting with peace and purpose is *trust-based obedience. In other words, the key to unlocking genuine, heartfelt obedience is a relationship of love and trust.* Before we can explore the obedience side of things—that is, what respect, discipline, and collaboration look like in this new parenting paradigm—we have to understand the importance of *trust* to the equation. More and more, research reveals that our bodies are created to thrive in relationship.

This starts in the womb. In many ways, the experience of the mother is inherently the experience of the child, and that directly affects how the child develops. Put another way, if the mother has experienced trauma within her pregnancy, it has the potential to affect the physical development of her unborn baby's brain. Even if an infant receives optimal nutrition and physical care, if affection, attachment, and connection are lacking, the child's physical and neurological development could be compromised.[1]

This basic need for connection doesn't diminish as the child grows. Whereas newborns' need for attachment is quite clear from their total dependence, toddlers are equally in need—but because they have the ability to walk and physically separate from their caregivers, that need for attachment looks different. This secure attachment with caregivers is integral to their healthy emotional and cognitive development. There is growing evidence that a child's attachment and connection with their parent offers protective benefits against risky behaviors in adolescence and mental health disorders, and it has the potential to positively influence physical health throughout their lifetime.[2]

If the stakes seem high, in many ways, they are. If we do not securely attach to our caregivers, we develop an insecure attachment style, which manifests in childhood as unhealthy attempts to meet our needs. Our bodies are hardwired to get connection any way they can—even if that means developing unhealthy behaviors or coping mechanisms. In adulthood, this can look like difficulty engaging in physical and emotional intimacy, struggling to form healthy relationships, or exhibiting unpredictable or inconsistent behavior with those we're closest to.

Craving Community

The very first page of the Bible speaks about how God created humans in His image (Genesis 1:27). Theologians have contemplated the precise meaning of "the image of God" for centuries. What is it specifically about us as humans that reflects God? This is an important question that deserves our thoughtful consideration, especially as it relates to attachment.

As Christians, we believe that God is not a solitary being; He is Father, Son, and Holy Spirit existing in eternal community. The Father, Son, and Spirit are united and connected as one, ever loving, ever giving love to one another, and ever receiving love from one another.[3] It is no surprise, then, that humans are made with a deep need for relationship, both with God and with each other. The bond of attachment between mothers and infants is *designed* to be strong, a reflection of God's own image so that we can flourish within a community of connection and companionship.[4]

Through the lens of attachment, we see that neuroscience and Scripture sing the same song. When a child feels connected to their parent, the self-preservation center of their brain is relaxed, signaling to their body that all is well. This means that, because their stress response is not activated, they are actually more receptive to learning and feel safe enough to develop new skills and improve their judgment. They won't always get it right, of course—but, no matter what, we can ground ourselves in the beautiful truth that our relationships with these little image bearers are imperfect reflections of the divine relationships. When we connect with our children, we get a glimpse of God.

Breaking—and Restoring—Connection

For decades, time-outs have been offered as an alternative to spanking. Child-rearing experts suggested isolating a child for a short period of time with the belief that removing attention from the child for bad behavior would decrease the behavior. And while that makes sense on the surface, recent research shows that relational pain (being rejected or neglected by a caregiver or loved one) can impact the brain the same way physical pain does. Humans were designed by God as relational beings. He wired us for connection, and that need can be heightened in times of distress. It is through the comfort and closeness of someone who loves and cares for us that we are able to regulate and calm down. Psychiatrist Daniel Siegel and psychotherapist Tina Payne Bryson explain how time-outs can backfire:

When the parental response is to isolate the child, an instinctual psychological need of the child goes unmet. In fact, brain imaging shows that the experience of relational pain—like that caused by rejection—looks very similar to the experience of physical pain in terms of brain activity.[5]

Emotional neglect involves inattentiveness to a child's emotional and developmental needs. It can be challenging to think of time-outs as isolation or emotional neglect. Yet those behaviors that cause us to threaten a time-out are almost always connected to unmet physical, emotional, or sensory needs; missing skills that our children haven't mastered yet; or unrealistic expectations from us as parents.

We're not here to judge or shame parents. We have Facebook memories that pop up each year reminding us of when our young toddler had to sit in a naughty chair. Emotional neglect was the furthest thing from our minds! Yet we were parenting in ways that were contrary to how God designed our children to live and to learn.

Looking back on my own birth experience with Ezra, I now have so much compassion for that worried new mama. Yes, the attachment science is true, but also true is the resilience of the God-given bond between mother and child. And even more powerful than that is the restorative, redemptive work that Christ does in and through His people. Attachment may be the proverbial tie that binds, but grace is the thread that weaves a lifelong story, a tapestry of restoration and redemption.

If your birthing and early motherhood story is like mine, or if you're an adoptive parent or have had experiences in parenting that have you wondering if strong and secure attachment with your child is possible, take heart. The God-given bond between a mother and child is powerfully resilient. God is always holding our stories and is eager to write His theme of reconciliation into them. And redemption will always lead to intentional and purposeful connection.

Connection in Action

Establishing connection and trust with our children enables us to confidently lead them to intuitively have faith in our leadership. Our kids can experience the joy of genuine obedience that springs from a trusting heart that is full of love. This trust is the foundation that makes the rest of our parenting workable.

If being securely attached to us as parents is how God made our little image bearers to thrive, how can we put that into practice? Perhaps you've been reading this chapter and thinking, *This all sounds so nice, David and Amanda, but it's not real life. I spend time with my kids, but they still misbehave. We can't just let them get away with bad behavior, can we?* If so, let us be the first to say: Your concerns are valid.

But what if we could honor the image of God in our children, keep them securely attached in their relationship to us as their parents, and *still* correct wrong behavior?

It's possible! Parenting with Jesus as our model gives us insight into how to respond with gentleness and peace (empowered by the Holy Spirit) when our children disobey, have tantrums, or are defiant and willful. Remembering to "connect *before* you correct"[6] helps us stay rooted in our goal of using Scripture and neuroscience to help our children flourish. Even repeating the phrase to ourselves in a difficult moment can serve as an anchor point, bringing us back to the truth that our children are wired to receive correction best when they feel connected to their parents. It is through the comfort and closeness of someone who loves and cares for them that they are best—and most efficiently!—able to regulate and calm down.

- Empathize with your child.
- Enter their world and get curious.
- Offer a hug or snuggle.
- Use nonverbal communication to let them know they are seen and understood.
- Invite them to swing, color, or dance with you.

It's not always easy, especially when your kids are in the middle of a meltdown or tantrum. If your go-to reaction is to control or force compliance, to become aggressive or loud, or to demand obedience, you aren't alone. If gentleness seems like an ultimate but unattainable goal, we've been there. Unlearning unhelpful parenting strategies takes time, and it can be quite an emotional process. But take comfort in knowing this: The Spirit of God dwells in you and is working with you to gently and graciously mold you into the image of His Son.

Try some of the following helpful practices to increase connection and peace within your home.

Gentle firmness

In the New Testament, we counted more than twenty-five commands for followers of Jesus to be gentle, kind, patient, and show honor to others. From responding to sin (Galatians 6:1) to resolving conflict (2 Timothy 2:23-26), from defending one's faith (1 Peter 3:15-16) to interacting with the world (Titus 3:1-2), gentleness is an irreplaceable and essential quality of those who bear the image of God and the name of Christ.

Proverbs 15:1 lends ancient wisdom for modern parents, especially for those exceptionally difficult moments: "A gentle answer turns away anger." Jesus-centered parenting means responding to your child's behavior with a gentle tone of voice. We don't mean baby talk or ultrasweet and flowery words. In the original Hebrew, the word that is translated *gentle* in Proverbs 15:1 carries with it the connotation of tenderness and nurturing. This distinction reminds us that our discipline and teaching of our children should be done with a posture of peace, nurturing, and tenderness. This takes a tremendous amount of strength of character and will!

When you must hold a limit or boundary with your child, rather than becoming harsh and forceful, practice gentle firmness. Empathize and help them with their struggle even as you hold the limit with compassionate confidence.

> For toddlers, this might sound like, "You are so sad to leave the park. I understand. I'm going to carry you to the car because it is time to go."
>
> For young children, this might sound like, "I can tell you're upset, and I want to understand why. Match my voice so I can understand you clearly."
>
> For tweens and teens, this might sound like, "This is important to you, and I want to understand it better. Let's take a break and go for a walk. We can come back to this once we've both calmed down."

Co-regulation, connection, communication

Our needs for connecting and regulating are as different as our fingerprints. You may even experience this in your own family. Sharing a warm smile and a deep energy between each other while working side by side on separate projects builds connection for some people, while others require deep, heartfelt conversations or shared fun to nurture their bond.

Our boys are the perfect example: Ezra's go-to calming strategy is to sit very still and take deep, slow breaths. But if we asked Elijah to do this, it would backfire—emphasis on fire! He prefers to move his body in big, bold ways, and as you might imagine, teaching him how to do that safely was quite an adventure.

As parents, we're often already attuned to our children's unique personalities and temperaments, but it can be easy to forget their unique needs for connection and regulation in the heat of the moment. Even if we're still learning how to be better attuned, one thing that can be transformative in the midst of a meltdown is how *we* show up.

Similar to the posture of peace from chapter 2, when you sense a difficult moment brewing, you can try following three simple steps to bring a measure of tenderness to a tense situation:

Co-regulate ➡ Connect ➡ Communicate

It can be easy to jump straight to communicate—after all, doesn't a child need to know that their behavior is unacceptable? But as we explained earlier, in the moment, the child's fear response is likely activated, so they're not fully capable of learning the important lesson we want them to learn. Instead, we work *with* what we know about the way God designed our children and their nervous systems rather than against it.

First, we co-regulate; that is, we move toward our child in an attempt to harmonize their dysregulated nervous system with our calm nervous system. While this doesn't necessarily require physical touch, some children find it especially comforting to have a gentle hand placed on their shoulder or to be given a warm hug in the midst of their struggle. Simply sitting side by side can prove to be co-regulating for the child who isn't as receptive to touch.

Remember, the goal here is only to be a safe and calming presence; no words are required (we know, it's so hard!). Draw on some of the resources we've explored for strengthening your inner peace: Take deep breaths, with exhales longer than your inhales; reflect on the lyrics of your favorite worship song; intentionally soften your face and your body. Slowly, these practices will help bring your child's nervous system back to a state of mutual, shared calm.

Next, we connect. Connecting with a child helps their brain recognize that they are safe and all is well in their world. You might think of it like this: Co-regulation prepares their mind for learning how to do better next time, and connection prepares their heart. What this looks like in the moment will vary based on your child's needs and the situation that led to escalation, but validating and empathizing with their struggle is always a good place to start.

Finally, we begin to communicate. Communicating with your child helps them become familiar and comfortable with tools and strategies they can use to calm their brains and bodies. With a spirit of understanding and compassion, we hold any urge to shame or blame and focus on instilling our family's values, gently guiding them on how they can do differently next time.

Take my (Amanda's) recent experience as an example of how to move through these three steps. We had some friends over one morning, and their son, who was newly two, was just not having it. I wasn't sure whether he'd gotten up entirely too early or whether this was his typical morning nap time, but one thing was clear: He was starting to lose it.

His big sister was nearby, clearly worried. I knelt down a few feet away from him and opened my arms. "Do you need a hug, buddy?" I asked in a low, soft voice. He waddled toward me, crying loudly.

As I scooped him up, I held him close and didn't say a word, instead focusing on my own inner calm. After a minute or two, his crying shifted from a wail of despair to something more akin to discontent.

When I noticed the shift in his body, I asked, "Do you like to play I Spy?" His eyes lit up. He nodded his head through his tears. "I spy with my little eye . . . something blue!" I said, and he eagerly looked around.

His big sister piped up, "I don't think he knows many colors yet." That didn't stop him from guessing anyway.

After three rounds of the "That's a good guess" I Spy, he started to pull away from me. As clearly as a disheveled toddler can muster, he stated, "I done crying now." After I set him back on his feet, he toddled over to a ball and started playing with it, even as he rubbed his hands across his face in an attempt to wipe away the tears.

Now, of course, it doesn't always happen this easily. But do you see the connection in action?

Co-regulate—A hug and holding was all this little guy needed. No words. Just calm presence.

Connect—Even though he wasn't quite ready for I Spy, he was up for a bit of playfulness as soon as the meltdown cycle started to wind down.

Communicate—He's only two years old, but he didn't need to wait for me to communicate with him. He volunteered that he was done crying and was ready to move on to the next thing without me having to say a word about it.

As your children grow and become less dependent on you for co-regulation, you can gently redirect them by both acknowledging their deep feelings and providing an opportunity to try again. Second chances (and sometimes third and fourth chances) that are offered in a calm and neutral tone are a powerful way to help little ones learn how to communicate hard things with respect and honor.

"It sounds like your frustration is talking. You won't be frustrated forever. Do you want help calming down, or do you want to be alone?"

"That sounds like your anger talking. I know this is important to you, and it is important to me too. Let's take a break until you are ready to talk."

"You must be so upset to say that. You have the freedom to say hard things as long as you're respecting yourself and others. Do you want to take a break, or try again right now?"

"Whoa! I can tell you're really upset. I want to hear you out. Will you try that again and speak plainly so I'm sure I understand what's going on?"

"I can tell this is important to you. I want to hear what you have to say. Why don't you try again with your regular voice."

"We're both feeling frustrated right now. Let's take a few minutes to reset, and then we can come back and find a solution that works for both of us."

Connection on Purpose: Magic Moments

Magic moments are intentional "special time" between a child and a parent or caregiver in which they engage in child-led connection and play for five to fifteen minutes.

How to get started

- Commit to five minutes at least three days per week (increase time and frequency, up to fifteen minutes per day, if it is possible for your family).
- Before your magic moments, explain to your child that they get special time with Mom or Dad. The only rule is that they are in charge!
- Set a visual timer.
- Let your child lead!
- If possible, when the timer goes off, finish the flow of play.

A few guidelines

To ensure your time together is as meaningful and life-giving to your children as possible, follow these best practices:

- child-led activities
- no phones
- no siblings
- no correcting unless absolutely necessary (for safety)
- no criticizing

It's Never Too Late

The journey of connection and attachment with our precious children is a profound and complex one, filled with both joy and challenges, moments of epic brilliance and moments of intense failure. You may find yourself haunted by the worry that you have made too many mistakes or failed to establish a secure attachment early enough in your relationship with your child. We certainly have.

The transformative power of love—both our love for our children and God's love for us—cannot be understated. God is a God of reconciliation, restoration, and redemption. Just as God extends endless grace to us, we can extend grace to ourselves and our children.

No parent is perfect. And it's helpful to recognize that, while consistent secure attachment is important, "good enough" parenting is often truly adequate. Children are remarkably resilient, often more easily capable of forgiveness and growth than we adults are. Our mistakes can serve as opportunities for learning and growth, fostering deeper connections with our children as we model humility, vulnerability, and the willingness to repair and make amends. Our imperfections as parents do not define us or hinder the possibility of deep connection with our children. Instead, they provide opportunities for growth, healing, and *renewed* connection.

It is never too late to forge a secure bond with your child. Parenting with gentleness and peace is not a linear path but a dynamic and complex relationship that unfolds over time. Each moment presents an opportunity to strengthen connection, nurture attachment, and create a safe and loving environment for trust to flourish.

Reflection Questions

1. Recall a moment of profound connection with your child. How did that interaction make you feel? How can you intentionally cultivate more of these bonding moments?

2. The chapter provides examples of connecting before correcting. How can you adapt these ideas to your family's unique dynamics and interests? Consider one practical way you can implement the "connect" step into your parenting routine.

3. In the context of Christian parenting, how does the concept of secure attachment align with Jesus' teaching and example? How might viewing the concept of secure attachment through a spiritual lens impact your parenting approach and the way you guide your child through challenges?

6

Trust-Based Obedience

Our firstborn, Ezra, was a really easygoing child and, for the most part, pretty compliant. Our second born, on the other hand . . . Have you seen the meme that says something like, "The first-born child makes parents think they know what they're doing, and the second born proves they don't"? That pretty much sums it up for us.

Their different personalities were evident even before birth. During the later part of my pregnancy with Ezra, I could gently push him off my rib, and he'd quickly adjust and find a new cozy spot. Elijah? When I'd gently but firmly give him a little push to the side, he'd kick or punch back as if to say, "Excuse me? You're intruding on *my* space, ma'am!"

Their unique temperaments were evident throughout toddlerhood as well. Ezra was about two and a half when he put himself in our "naughty chair" because he didn't want to follow directions. Elijah, however, had no use for this chair and flat-out refused to sit in it of his own free will.

It's not altogether surprising that Elijah's need for independence at any cost tempted us to give up nonpunitive, peacemaking parenting. All of our tried-and-true gentle techniques didn't have anywhere *near* the same effect on him as they had on his brother.

To be fair, Elijah comes from a long line of strong-willed, strong-minded, and strong-spirited people. We know exactly where these qualities come from—both sides of the family! And, of course, we love, honor, and value those strengths in our boy. But we'd be lying if we told you that life with a strong-willed toddler and a sensitive preschooler was easy. It was one of the most difficult seasons of our lives.

Try as we might—and did we ever try!—nothing seemed to "work." It felt like everything we had ever learned about what it means to raise a God-loving, well-adjusted child was totally wrong. After all, doesn't the Bible *tell* children they have to obey?

Well, yes and no.

Obedience Matters

Obey. It's the four-letter word of childhood.

Our children arrive in this world completely dependent on us to meet their needs. As babies, that exclusive focus on their own needs is critical to their survival. They have to sleep, they have to eat, they have to poop—and they need us to help with all of it. As they grow and become walking, talking toddlers, that self-centeredness doesn't magically disappear, but it looks a lot less like absolute dependence and a lot more like exerting their opinions—at all times. They've suddenly realized that there's a difference between "me" and "you."

This is when teaching obedience typically becomes a focal point of child-rearing. It is also at this point, just when our young disciples are first recognizing and experimenting with their own free will, that parents are tempted to throw in the towel and give up on implementing this peacemaking parenting perspective in their homes. Of course they are! It can be exhausting—and feel anything but peaceful—to raise a desperately independent child. (Ask us how we know.)

Not only that, but helping our children learn to obey is a valid desire—leading to harmonious family life now and the ability to listen to, collaborate with, and honor others later on. The toddler who just made mud pies has to take a bath before nap time, whether he wants to or not. The preschooler needs to find something better to do than annoying and frustrating his sister until she finally hits him. The grade-schooler needs to read short books each week to build the reading skills she'll need to demonstrate months from now. As parents, our goals for obedience are often really good, with future benefits in mind!

When we commit to parenting with peace and purpose, we do not surrender ourselves (and our sanity!) to disobedience and accept that our children will rule our homes with their strong wills and ideas and never listen to our own. Obedience matters—it matters to your family, and it matters to God.

So why does helping your child find the path to obedience seem so hard? Perhaps because we tend to overlook the foundation of obedience, which—according to Jesus—is even more important than obedience itself. So often in our quest to raise good, godly, and obedient children, we as parents miss the foundational piece—the key that unlocks true obedience: trust.

At this point you may be thinking, *That's all well and good, David and Amanda. I want my child to trust me. But I also want my child to willingly put on their pants when I ask.*

How *is* trust related to obedience, anyway? To find out, let's look at that well-known command from Paul: "Children, obey your parents in the Lord, because this is right" (Ephesians 6:1).

There's context in these eleven words that we as modern readers of Scripture don't always get. "In the Lord" is simple and easy for us to read, and we know that it means something about Jesus. The phrase "Jesus is Lord" is so common that it appears on bumper stickers, bookmarks, T-shirts, church banners, and of course viral-worthy social media memes. But that wasn't the case in the first-century Roman Empire. To the church in Ephesus, the ubiquitous phrase was "Caesar is Lord."

Obedience to Caesar was unquestioned and nonnegotiable. The Roman Empire had risen by maintaining peace through any means. Its greatness was forged through relentless violence as it ruthlessly defeated and subjugated numerous civilizations. Because of their thirst for dominance and power, the Roman legions established authority through force, thereby bringing order to the conquered regions. This resulted in the Pax Romana, or "Roman peace," a period of relative peace and stability throughout their vast territories. Force and intimidation were used to quell internal conflicts and suppress dissent, but at the expense of the conquered people's freedom and autonomy. The notion of peace through violence highlights the historical reality that worldly peace has often been imposed through strength and power.

So when Paul writes, "Children, obey your parents in the Lord," the Christians in Ephesus would have had an immediate context. But they also would have noted the resulting contrast, one we don't usually think about: Jesus and Caesar are not the same kind of lord.

Lord Caesar executed his enemies—real and perceived, while Lord Jesus died for His enemies. Lord Caesar demanded compliance through oppression and threats, while Lord Jesus invited relationship and partnership through service and love. Lord Caesar leveraged his power to force obedience; Lord Jesus extended a grace that compelled obedience. Lord Caesar oppressed; Lord Jesus freed. Lord Caesar demanded repentance through threat; Lord Jesus brought repentance through kindness.

If we as parents think Ephesians 6:1 means we should force, coerce, or harshly demand obedience of our children, we are confusing Lord Jesus with lord Caesar. Obedience "in the Lord" is obedience that is born out of kindness (Romans 2:3-4), love (John 14:15), and trust (1 John 4:18).

As we start recalibrating our understanding of obedience in the Lord Jesus, perhaps we should examine what He says about obedience.

Jesus-Centered Perspective

For many, obedience comes with an implied adjective: "immediate." We want our kids to get dressed *right now*. We want them to clean up their toys *right now*. We want them to behave in public *right now*.

Of course, when it comes to life-or-death safety, immediate compliance is vital. But outside of that, does obedience *require* immediate action? You might have heard it said—or even preached—that delayed obedience is disobedience.

There's just one big problem with that view—Jesus' own words tell us the opposite.

In Matthew 21:28-32, Jesus tells a parable about a father and his two sons. The father goes to each of them and asks them to go work in the vineyard. One son initially refuses to go but later changes his mind, ultimately deciding to follow his father's request. The other son immediately says he will go work but doesn't follow through.

WHEN IS IMMEDIATE OBEDIENCE WARRANTED?

Because young children are immature, impulsive, and unaware of danger, there are times when we as parents will require immediate obedience—particularly when it comes to protecting our children's lives.

Fear-based compliance does have a God-designed purpose: survival. When it comes to safety, being *proactive* is much better than being *reactive*:

- Have a plan that prevents most dangerous situations altogether. (You say, "You may ride your tricycle on the sidewalk" rather than allowing your child to drive it down the driveway where they may lose control and wind up in the street.)
- Create a specific cue that indicates danger (whistle, snap, loud voice, etc.).

Of course, accidents still happen. But when you reserve your urgent, loud, and harsh reactions for the occasions when God intended them to be used (to ensure survival), His plan works remarkably well.

After telling this parable to the leaders of Israel, Jesus asks, "Which of the two did his father's will?" (Matthew 21:31). Did both sons disobey their father?

It may seem so at first. After all, neither son immediately and willingly jumps to the task. But the crowd answers—and Jesus agrees—that there *is* an obedient son: the one who initially disobeys but eventually does what his father asked. It's not about who initially disobeys or who says they will obey, but who ultimately does the will of God. It's not about being perfect or simply saying we follow God. Instead, what matters is whether we are willing to change our minds (in other words, to repent) and follow Him.

For Jesus, delayed obedience is still counted—and honored—as obedience. This is good news—for everyone! If God never recognized our delayed obedience as obedience, we would be in a really bad way. It's impossible to instantly obey every single command found in the Bible or every leading of the Holy Spirit. The whole gospel rests on God's patient grace. Jesus never requires perfection from His people. He only asks that we follow Him.

Jesus also makes abundantly clear in the parable of the unforgiving servant (Matthew 18:21-35) that He expects those who have been forgiven much to forgive the sins of others. Shall we receive God's mercy and grace for our disobedience to Him while not offering the same to our children? He gives us as parents the opportunity to teach our children about God's grace by extending that same grace to them.

When we adopt the "delayed obedience is disobedience" view, we lay a heavier burden on our children than God designed them—or anyone—to bear. And we want to be clear: We know that most parents aren't issuing capricious commands and harshly punishing children for the slightest hesitation. Most parents give commands and expectations that are rooted in their love and care for their children. But if we are to parent as peacemakers in our homes, we will shift our perspective toward a more gracious understanding of obedience, one that focuses on our children's hearts before their behavior.

The real goal of Christian parenting is not simply children who obey but children who *want* to obey, even if it takes them a little time to choose the path of obedience.

THE DANGER OF DEMANDING IMMEDIATE OBEDIENCE

Something to consider: Teaching children immediate obedience or compliance can inadvertently create fertile ground for abuse and exploitation. While it is important for children to learn self-discipline and respect for others, an excessive emphasis on unquestioning obedience to authority can hinder their critical thinking skills, obstruct their learning of wisdom, and compromise their ability to assert boundaries.

We want our children to develop the necessary skills to recognize and resist manipulation and abusive behavior. Encouraging open communication and independent thinking, along with empowering children to voice their concerns, can help create a safe environment that promotes their overall well-being.

It Starts—Again—with Us

Teaching a child to *want* to obey is far harder and takes much longer than just getting them to immediately do what we ask.

For me (David), this comes into clear focus when I'm staring at a full dishwasher.

Have you noticed that small children create a disproportionately large number of dirty dishes? After one too many nights staying up to corral and wash all the dishes after the kids went to bed, Amanda and I thought we might try to involve the boys in this chore. Every day, they would contribute to our family by unloading the dishwasher and putting the clean dishes away. With lots of coaching, plenty of silliness, and loads of practice, they eventually became capable of emptying the dishwasher. Most days.

But one day, Elijah just wasn't having it. He did not want to put away the dishes. He wanted to play. He had been reminded a couple of times that it needed to be done, but he always had something better to do.

By now the afternoon was wearing on, the breakfast and lunch dishes were still piled in the sink, and cooking supper was going to be a challenge. So I went looking for the laggard. I found him in his room. After asking what he was playing, I listened with interest before saying, "Hey, will you come join me in the kitchen?"

He followed me there, where I pointed to the dishwasher and said, "The dishwasher still needs to be emptied."

Elijah looked straight at me. "I don't want to."

Staying calm, I said, "Bud, I need the dishwasher emptied so I can fill it back up with our dirty dishes. Otherwise I won't be able to fix supper in a few minutes."

"I don't care." He didn't say it to be intentionally disrespectful. He was simply stating a fact: He wasn't concerned about the dishwasher or the upcoming dinnertime plans.

I stood there looking at him. We were at an impasse. Neither asking nor logic had moved him. My options were now trying to make him do it (thereby inviting a power struggle), just doing the thing myself (and letting him get away with shirking responsibility), or getting creative to find another way. I decided to switch gears.

"Hey, bud, are you hungry?"

"I don't know," he grumbled. By now he was sitting on the floor in front of the dishwasher, arms crossed, head low.

Reader, he was hungry.

Throughout the Bible, Jesus feeds people. A lot. Much of His teaching and discipling takes place around a table or as a basket of miracle fish is being passed around to a hungry crowd (see Matthew 14:13-21). For parents, Goldfish crackers might be as close to miracle loaves and fish as we can get. And judging by the indescribable amounts of Goldfish we found in the back of our car when the boys were toddlers, there's a chance that God does, in fact, still perform the miracle of multiplying fish. But I digress. In any event, I've learned to take a cue from Jesus to feed our tiny disciples often—*really often*. It almost always improves the situation.

Pulling a snack from the fridge, I sat at the table and waited. A minute later, I watched Elijah look at the dishwasher. Next he looked at me. Then he stood and came to eat a snack with me at the table.

I'll admit, I was still a bit frustrated, and I was tempted to launch into a lecture on the importance of everyone contributing to the family, how unloading the dishwasher is easy, and how he'd probably spent more time fighting me over unloading the dishwasher than he would have just doing it. Instead, we sat together at the table eating and talking about whatever was on his mind.

When Elijah finished his snack, he jumped up and began emptying the dishwasher. No prompting, nagging, or lecture was needed. He just got right to work with a skip in his step and authentic joy in

CO-REGULATE, CONNECT, COMMUNICATE: A REAL-LIFE EXAMPLE

In the last chapter, we talked about building connection and defusing tension through the three-step process of co-regulating, connecting, and communicating the correction. Did you see how it played out with Elijah when he wouldn't empty the dishwasher?

- I co-regulated by meeting his physical need for food.
- I connected by following his lead and engaging in the conversation he was interested in.
- In this case, he self-corrected without further prompting, though if he had still been resistant, I would have offered to come alongside him to empty the dishwasher together. (To understand more about helping our children with obedience, check out the Quick Reference Guide on page 221.)

his heart. All it took was a little bit of fuel and some trust-building connection, and he chose to follow the path of obedience.

Our dishwasher revolution is a small, everyday example, but it highlights an important truth: The key to unlocking our children's desire to obey is often found in our *own* actions. When we look back to Ephesians 6, we see the apostle Paul driving this point home.

As Paul closes his letter to the Ephesians, he goes through a list of commands for six different groups of people (Ephesians 5:22–6:9). Paul didn't just pull this approach out of thin air. Ethical teaching in the first century often included a set of "household codes" that told the various members of a large (wealthy) household how to act. Specifically, these codes told the head of the household the rules he should enforce with his wife, children, and slaves.[1] Instead of repeating admonitions common to the culture of his day, Paul does something radical—he addresses each member of the household directly. He tells the wife, children, and slaves how to act toward the head of the house while also telling the husband/father/master explicitly how he should relate to his wife, children, and slaves.[2] This is Paul subverting our upside-down world and starting to put it right side up, starting with the family.

For parents, Paul has a pertinent instruction: "Fathers, don't stir up anger in your children" (Ephesians 6:4). He drives home a similar point in Colossians. We love how it reads in the Amplified version:

> Fathers, do not provoke *or* irritate *or* fret your children [do not be hard on them or harass them], lest they become discouraged *and* sullen *and* morose *and* feel inferior *and* frustrated. [Do not break their spirit.]
> COLOSSIANS 3:21, AMPC

Together, Jesus and Paul elevate children to a place of honor in the home and family. It was a radical divergence from how children were treated at that time in human history. Their teaching, though given directly to first-century followers of Jesus, is, in some ways, still radical today. Over the years, we've had our fair share of people tell us that validating emotions and being aware of our children's feelings isn't biblical. Yet in the entirety of the New Testament, there are three commands given explicitly about parenting—and two of them are about our children's feelings.

- "Don't stir up anger in your children" (Ephesians 6:4).
- "Bring them up in the training and instruction of the Lord" (Ephesians 6:4).
- "Do not exasperate your children, so that they won't become discouraged" (Colossians 3:21).

Paying attention to our children's emotional well-being is not only good for their development but also helps prime them for obedience. When we are emotionally safe for our kids, they can fully trust us. And when we pair trust with honor, we see joyful desire for obedience emerge in our children.

But Shouldn't They Honor *Us*?

Absolutely. Let's take another look at Ephesians 6:1, where Paul commands children to "obey your parents in the Lord." Unfortunately, this verse is often taken outside of its full context, ushering in a host of incorrect applications antithetical to Christ's heart for parenting.

For example, this passage is often interpreted to include an implicit command: Parents should *force* their children to obey. If we don't make children do what we ask, how will they ever learn? However, if we take the verse in its context (Ephesians 5:22–6:9), we see its true meaning revealed. Does the directive "Wives, submit to your husbands" (Ephesians 5:22) contain an implicit command that husbands should *force* their wives to submit? Or does the command "Husbands, love your wives" (Ephesians 5:25) implicitly mean that wives should *force* their husbands to love them? In fact, the commands that Paul gives in this passage are delicately intertwined—and if force is any part of the equation, one of the commands is being broken. If a husband forces his wife to follow the command to submit, he breaks the command given to him to love her as himself. If a master uses fear and trembling to force his slaves to obey, he breaks the command given to him not to use threats (see Ephesians 6:5-9). If we force our children to follow the command to obey, we break the command given to us not to stir up anger in them.

Our actions are just as important as our children's. When we shift our mindset to trust-based, peacemaking parenting, we seek to guide, not control, their choices and behavior.

Paul doesn't stop with obedience. Instead, he goes deeper,

taking us all the way back to the Ten Commandments. There the command is to honor our parents (Exodus 20:12). In Hebrew, the word *honor* includes much more than simple obedience; it evokes concepts of worthiness and respect. And it doesn't apply only to childhood; this commandment applies to our whole lives.

This is the root of true and joyful obedience: cultivating *mutual* honor and respect. Looking forward a few years (or decades), we hope and pray that our children will *share* our purpose and values and live them out with passion and excitement! This is what will persist long past the days of tucking them into bed every night. Obedience to parents is for a season, but honor is meant for a lifetime.

Teaching Trust-Based Obedience

Throughout our parenting journey we've had the opportunity to lock arms with other families who are shifting away from punitive discipline and short-term obedience to focus on building long-term relationships of honor and trust. Alyssa is one of those moms, and her three-year-old son, Colton, reminds us of our Elijah. Colton is spirited, strong-willed, and has fire deep in his soul, which easily spills out to everyone around him.

During a group-mentoring Zoom call, Alyssa brought up Colton's absolute refusal to pick up toys at the end of the day. "I don't understand it!" she said. "He's more than capable of taking everything out and playing with each toy in appropriate ways, and he knows where they go. But when it's time to put them away, he runs from the room screaming, 'Nooooo!'

"The thing is," she confided, "in that moment, I know all the things I *don't* want to do. I know I don't want to physically force him to pick up the toys; I know I don't want to threaten throwing the toys away; and I definitely know I don't want to just do it for him. But if I don't want to do any of those things, what options are left? I still feel stuck actually trying to decide what *to do*."

Even over Zoom, it was clear that Alyssa's vulnerability struck a chord with the other parents, and they voiced their agreement, shaking their heads in shared confusion. When it comes down to it, the nuts and bolts of trust-based obedience can be just plain *hard*.

I (Amanda) stepped in. "We've been there, Alyssa—and we know how helpless it feels. It's the opposite of the empowered parenting we desire! I wonder, instead of asking, 'How can I *make* my child obey?' whether you could consider asking yourself, 'How can I *help* my child obey?' I've found that, for me, the shift from *make* to *help* makes all the difference."

The beautiful thing about parenting in community is that you can gain ideas from others who have been there before. Encouraged by Alyssa's sharing, other parents began to swap experiences and ideas of how they moved through similar situations.

One mom chimed in and said she found that having set times throughout the day to put away toys helped her children not feel overwhelmed by a big mess at the end of the day. Another parent, with slightly older children, admitted that she found it necessary to minimize their toys and craft supplies so that the mess was manageable *for her* and her children. David reminded me of how we would get playful with Elijah in such moments, trying to allow him to take charge of the situation by making him the expert. We've even heard of dads picking up their toddlers and preschoolers by their feet and pretending they're vacuum cleaners as they playfully work together to "suck up" all the toys.

By the end of the call, Alyssa had a plan for Colton and his toys—one that didn't resort to threats or punishment but that would meet him where he was and support him through the learning of an important life skill.

Two weeks later she updated us: "Every evening when it's time to put away his toys I pretend to be a forgetful opera singer. I use the silliest voice to sing about the toys and all the wrong places they go, and without fail, Colton bursts into giggles and 'corrects' my mistakes. It took a few tries because he was skeptical at first, but now cleanup time is a moment of connection and fun for both of us. We work together, and I'm learning to accept whatever his best is that day instead of expecting him to do it perfectly or completely every time just because I told him to."

It seems counterintuitive, but helping our children obey doesn't have to mean standing over them and coercing them to comply. It doesn't mean threatening them so they do what we say. It doesn't mean exerting our authority so they fear our judgment, or shaming them so they feel bad enough to do what we asked. Instead, much like the Helper promised by Jesus who indwells and empowers us, we can come alongside our children to empower them as we

help them pick up the toys,
help them get in the car seat,
help them practice folding their laundry,
help them put the scissors down,
help them name their feelings,
and help them take their jumpiness outside to the trampoline
    instead of on the couch.

When we help in this way, we aren't sliding into permissive parenting or letting our kids "get away" with anything. Instead, we are meeting them where they are—in their current emotional, mental, and physical capacities and their current stages of brain development—and giving them what their little hearts need most.

We've found a number of other practical ways we can help our children to obey.

Offer choices

One way to disarm power struggles is to hand over some control to the one who feels powerless. Offering choices doesn't give children free rein to rule the roost! It uses wide boundaries that work for the parent and give autonomy and free agency to the child.

For toddlers and preschoolers, this might sound like:

> "It's time to get ready for bed! Would you like to ride on my back to your room to get your jammies on, or would you like to have an animal parade to go brush your teeth?"
>
> "It's almost time to leave the park. Would you like to leave now and race to the car, or would you like to pick one more thing to do?"
>
> "It's time to get dressed! Do you want to put on your shirt or your pants first?"

As children develop the ability to think critically, they'll start to see that the options you give are within a boundary they may not like. This is a great opportunity to invite collaboration. With grade-schoolers, this might sound like:

> "I'm going to make rosemary pork chops for supper. What vegetables would you like for a side?"
>
> "I'm not okay with slime being in your room. You can play with it at the table or on the family room floor. Does that work for you, or do you have a different idea?"
>
> "The living room needs to be tidied! I see toys, shoes, and pillows that need to be put away. What's your plan?"

Ask questions

Children aren't robots. We can't expect them to go through life following commands and then launch them into the real world with basically no problem-solving skills. Instead of giving directives all the time, switch things up by asking questions.

For toddlers and preschoolers, this might sound like:

"It's almost time to go! What do you need to do to be ready?"
"The crayons are all over the floor! What can we do with them instead?"
"It's snowing outside, and you don't want to wear your coat. What should we do in case you get cold?"

For grade-schoolers, asking questions is a great way to help them think through situations. Often, asking about the potential outcome can help them reach their own conclusions. Once they reach the tween years, though, these types of questions can come across as condescending, so asking, "What's your plan?" might be an option when you notice leading questions aren't landing the way they used to.

Keep the list of nonnegotiables short

Sometimes we want to help our kids learn obedience by giving them lots of rules, commands, and expectations to follow. We should know this is a recipe for disaster—after all, Adam and Eve had only one rule and they couldn't manage to obey it. In cultivating joyful, heartfelt obedience, keep your list of nonnegotiables as short as you can. In our family, the nonnegotiables were always related to health and safety. When it came to navigating parking lots safely when our boys were toddlers or preschoolers, there were two choices: hold a grown-up's hand or ride in a shopping cart. No exceptions. And when it came to eating meals after helping Daddy feed and water the cows, washing hands was a must. Keep in mind that the boundaries, limits, and expectations you have for your child change at a rapid pace. It is natural that they will consistently test boundaries—after all, they're constantly learning where new ones are!

Becoming a Channel of Mercy

A trusting relationship may be the key to lifelong honor, but first it has to survive the years of testing and disobedience. When our toddler is in the middle of a meltdown because they absolutely do not want to take a bath, are we just going to look them in the eye, say, "Trust me," and watch them magically hop in the tub? Not likely.

A child's delayed obedience is ultimately an opportunity for *us*—to practice patience, model self-control, demonstrate kindness, and allow the fruit of the Spirit to flourish in us. Instead of thinking, *My child is disobeying me*, consider this small mindset shift: *My child isn't obeying me yet.* That last word opens so much beautiful potential for your child—and for you as well. When you recognize that they aren't obeying *yet*, you can consider your role in the situation:

- *Are my expectations reasonable?*
- *Am I acting in a way that invites and nurtures genuine obedience, or am I simply trying to demand compliance?*
- *Am I trying to forge peace or force peace?*
- *What do they need help learning or doing, and how can I provide the gentle, Christlike guidance they need in this moment?*
- *Are there unmet needs that I can help satisfy?*
- *Does it serve them better for me to model the request myself or to help them?*

Asking yourself these questions—especially in the heat of the moment—can provide the perspective you need to ground yourself in your new parenting values and pivot you toward your children instead of away from them. They need you to be a parent who lovingly guides their behavior until they're mature enough to make wise decisions on their own. You can see further than the current moment. You have wisdom to help your children navigate life. Even when your children can't see why your plan is likely the only workable solution, they still need the security of your confident leadership. And so, use delayed obedience as an opportunity to disciple, mentor, and teach your children through Christlike love. Give them permission to practice and fail within the safety of your unconditional love. Extend to them the radical grace God extends to you, and in this, you will become a channel of mercy to your children.

A Harvest of Wisdom

When each of our boys started kindergarten, we purchased an adult-sized T-shirt with "Class of" and their high school graduation year proudly displayed across the front. On their first day of school, they donned the magnificently too-large shirt to take pictures, and every year since, we've photographed them wearing their shirt on the day a new school year starts. Watching them slowly grow into those shirts year after year has been surreal and sentimental.

Their first year wearing the "Class of" shirts, they looked like they were wearing dresses, the hem of the shirt falling well below their knees. The shirts were so oversized, in fact, that both of our boys had to stretch out their arms to each side so we could make out the text on the front. Otherwise the shirts folded over on themselves, concealing the most important part.

The next year, the shirts were still overwhelmingly too big. By second grade, the shoulders fit well enough that the boys no longer had to hold their arms out so we could see the text, but it wasn't until Ezra was going into fourth grade—after a significant growth spurt that summer—that we could actually visualize what he might look like wearing the shirt his senior year.

Our discipleship of our children is much like that oversized shirt. When they are young, we have big visions and dreams for them. Our expectations and hopes are larger than life, often too big for them to shoulder. While we snuggle their tiny bodies, we're keenly aware that we're not merely giving them a healthy childhood; we're trying to prepare them for healthy adulthood and all that entails.

Here's the thing, though: Often we expect our teaching, guidance, and discipline to help our kids grow into their future roles more quickly than possible. It's as if we can somehow hurry up their learning so they can grow more quickly into maturity. But this is as futile as trying to speed up their physical growth so they fit into adult-sized clothes more quickly!

God's plan and design for childhood development is good. When we place expectations on our children that He has not yet equipped them to fulfill, we risk burdening them with a load they cannot carry.

Biblical obedience is learned slowly but eventually reaps a harvest of wisdom. Earning their obedience by building trust is part of this process and should be a natural part of nurturing our children as they grow. Our children will truly need this good judgment throughout their lives. As they grow and mature, wisdom will help them discern their next steps—when a teacher seems unfair, when a struggling friend whose parents' marriage has fallen apart comes to them for help, or when they have a crush on someone who won't respect physical boundaries. The time to start sowing for this kind of wisdom is now, long before our children face consequential decisions that will change the course of their lives.

Reflection Questions

1. How does a deeper understanding of Jesus' approach to your *own* obedience to Him change your view of your child's obedience? With that understanding in mind, what are some practical ways you can encourage and reassert your unconditional love for your children?

2. Think about a current issue or conflict you are having with your child. How could you become a channel of God's mercy within that circumstance? How do you think that could change the dynamic?

3. Spend time reflecting on the visions and dreams you have for your children as fully developed adults. Who do you want them to be? What qualities do you want them to possess? Knowing that right now they are just children, what are some practical ways you can actively remind yourself of that truth?

Cultivating Respect in Conflict

We have the perfect plot of land for raising two active boys. Our little spot of earth includes eight acres of mostly pastureland but with plenty of trees for climbing and a picturesque fallen log over a dry creek bed at the very back of our property. With plenty of room for activity and imaginative play, we've enjoyed countless hours hunting dinosaurs, having Nerf wars, practicing soccer, and going on adventures.

This particular summer the boys were just old enough to tramp across our property by themselves in pursuit of the kind of shenanigans that forever remain just between brothers. But by July, the sun bore down as the relentless days turned into long weeks of near-record temperatures. The intense summer heat drove us indoors except for during the earliest parts of the morning. After that, the boys and I (Amanda) weren't even all that comfortable just sitting in the shade on our front porch. The heat pricked our skin, and the humidity . . . let's just say we might have been more comfortable if we'd been born with gills instead of lungs.

One morning Ezra and Elijah were busy at their LEGO table, building planes and spacecrafts piece by piece. I was in the kitchen getting ready to fix lunch when all the heat of a Texas summer exploded out of my boys. To this day I can't recall why things went sideways with them, but they both were hot with anger. Their fury came out loud and big, words flying, tempers flaring, and LEGO pieces going everywhere as each boy scrambled to protect his creations.

We were about halfway through what had been a difficult summer. Though we'd spent a few years working with our boys and teaching them how to navigate conflict with honor, respect, and nonviolent collaboration and communication, they'd been struggling to put all that practice into action in the heat of the moment. Their skirmishes weren't usually physical anymore, but they were loud and rarely productive.

Not only had I spent the past few years teaching my sons how to resolve conflict, but I'd also been working through my own parenting triggers, identifying them and learning new ways to respond. But my kids fighting over one LEGO piece when we quite literally have thousands of pieces is still one of my biggest struggles. And as the summer heat burned outside the house, it took everything I had to keep my cool inside our home. On this morning, chaos and calm were in an inescapable dance, but chaos was taking the lead. Despite my own irritation, I needed to find a way to change that. But that meant *I had to take the lead*. I had to bring peace straight into the middle of conflict.

I called a family meeting, grabbing blankets and pillows and tossing them on our living-room rug. I sat myself squarely in the middle so my boys could sit on either side of me. They needed physical distance between them. We sat quietly for a few minutes just breathing, and Ezra and Elijah slowly cozied up next to me as they calmed down. When I was fairly confident they would be able to speak without yelling, I asked each of them to tell me their side of the story.

Dear reader, I wish I could tell you what the conflict was about. I just remember it involved LEGO pieces. We talked through the conflict, found a solution, moved some LEGO pieces into another room so they could design and create in separate spaces, and I went back to fixing lunch. While I don't remember the particulars, I do remember that I stayed calm. Truly calm. This was the result of years of work—not just with our two sons but with myself.

The PEACE Plan

Cultivating a posture of respect in difficult moments is *so* hard. But these situations truly are some of the most critical moments of your parenting. You stand at a crossroads. Take one path, and you begin a tumultuous journey: You match your child's disrespect with your own, demanding they show you the respect you deserve. "You really need to drop the attitude *right now*," you snap, adding in a threatened consequence for good measure. While this path may get you to your desired destination more efficiently—your child falls in line and adjusts their attitude— it ultimately leads to unnecessary resentment, fear, and stress in your relationship.

The second path, at first glance, seems more laborious and absolutely less efficient: You choose to respond to your child's disrespect with the wisdom, maturity, and kindness you want to instill in them. You choose to model for them the behavior you expect. Rather than appealing to your authority as a parent and demanding respect, you cultivate trust and show them what honor looks like in action.

One of the most transformative helps we've found on the path to peace in moments of conflict is the PEACE Plan. I'd come up with it a few years before that summer and had been teaching it to Ezra and Elijah ever since.

This is how the PEACE Plan works. While it's effective for children, this is how David and I implement the plan as parents. In difficult moments we try our best to:

P = Pause

If pausing feels impossible, there's a reason for that. Researchers have found that your brain has just about half of a second to determine your reaction to the stimuli it receives.[1] This is a good gift because it enables you to react insanely fast in the face of an emergency or potential danger!

But it also means that you have to intentionally choose, and practice, pausing before you respond to your child's behaviors. (This is where scripting and practicing a response can be incredibly helpful, as discussed in chapter 5.)

If the situation isn't an emergency, don't treat it like one! Slow down, take a step back and a deep breath (or a few breaths), and remind yourself that you are safe, your child is safe, and your home is safe.

E = Evaluate

Evaluation is twofold: First, evaluate what is happening in *your* heart. What are your needs and feelings, and if they need to be communicated, how can you do that without making your child responsible for them? Second, evaluate the situation. Can you determine the events that led up to the conflict? What outside influences are playing a role in your child's behavior?

A = *Acknowledge*

Acknowledge what is going on underneath your child's behavior. As much as you can, put yourself in their shoes and try to see them as God sees them. He is not triggered by their immaturity; He designed them that way! What are their needs and feelings, and how can you validate them? What perspective or skills are they lacking? How can you help them practice missing skills and communicate their needs and emotions with honor and respect?

C = *Collaborate*

We suspect you have significantly more collaboration with your child than you realize; after all, you and your little one worked together to help him learn to walk, to help her learn how to say her first words, and to fill in the rhythms and routines of your days. The goal of collaboration is to meet the needs of both parent and child and to find a workable and mutually agreeable solution or plan. In order to do this, you have to know what your shared concerns, goals, expectations, and desires are. That's how you find common ground.

Here's what it might look like through the ages and stages of parenting:

> For toddlers and early preschoolers, as well as children who are nonverbal or not yet verbal, you may need to narrate the problem: "Both of you want to build with this green LEGO piece; is that right?"
>
> Then suggest a couple of solutions to their problem: "I see this other piece is the same shape, but yellow. I wonder if one of you could use the green LEGO and the other could use the yellow one?" or "Here's a bigger green piece. I wonder if one of your creations might be able to use this green LEGO instead?"

Using "I wonder" statements models curiosity and problem-solving, and it gives even young children the opportunity to think about how to find a mutually agreeable solution. And yes, it's true—they may not agree on an answer to the problem, and in some cases, you may need to put away the green LEGO piece until they're ready to find a solution that works for both of them, or until the moment of discord and fractious engagement has passed. That's reasonable and sometimes necessary, but we want to encourage you not to make that your first response. Instead, let that be one of your last options.

For elementary and grade-schoolers: If you've already laid a foundation of finding mutually agreeable solutions to problems, you can say something like, "It sounds like there's a problem to be solved together. I know you can find a solution, and if you need help I'll be in the laundry room." (If you don't feel like you can leave them alone to practice problem-solving for very long, stay within earshot so you can monitor their progress.) Remember that they're learning and practicing conflict resolution, so it isn't going to sound like a diplomatic negotiation in your living room. They might be a little louder than you'd hope, and their solution might not seem all that fair to you. Give them the freedom to practice imperfectly. Small progress toward a big-picture goal is a worthwhile endeavor.

If you haven't already coached them in conflict resolution, now's the time to start! Teach them the PEACE Plan—modifying it to more closely align with your family's values and goals—and start mentoring them in this valuable life skill.

With tweens and teenagers, you may find that practicing collaborative problem-solving happens between you and your child more than between siblings or peers. The process is the same: You express your concern or perspective and allow them to express theirs. Then look for a solution that will address both your concerns and is acceptable to each of you.

E = Empower

We focus on empowering our children to do better or choose differently in the future instead of punishing them for what has already happened. Empowering your child in this way requires wisdom, discernment, and your own ability to learn from mistakes. Are there boundaries that will help avoid this situation in the future? What skills need to be practiced? Are there emotional, physical, or sensory needs that can be met proactively in the future to minimize similar situations playing out?

When our boys were toddlers, they needed a lot of practice in learning to control their impulses—especially when it came to using their hands. Pinching, slapping, and hitting were instinctive reactions for both of them when they were upset, and so we taught them many strategies for using their hands safely. We used the game Simon Says and helped them learn to make a tight fist and then slowly open their hands so they could "feel" the tension leave their bodies. We found fun, creative, and skill-building ways to help them practice when they weren't agitated and then offered gentle (and painstakingly frequent) reminders when they were upset. This is also where future-facing consequences may come into play (see chapter 9).

The Pathway to Peace

Not long after sitting and talking with the boys about their altercation over LEGOs that hot summer morning, we gathered again, this time around the kitchen table. "I've noticed you guys are really struggling with solving problems and resolving conflict this summer," I said. "Have you noticed that?"

They nodded, a look of defeat on both of their faces.

"Do you remember our PEACE Plan? We've talked about it lots of times." For the longest time, this approach to conflict resolution seemed to be helping them. But this summer . . . there was something about this summer, and while I don't know what it was, I do know that bickering, fighting, arguing, and verbal attacks were frequent, and our PEACE Plan wasn't really being followed.

"Sort of," Ezra muttered. He wasn't really grumpy so much as he would've rather been talking about anything but this. I let it go and shared an idea with them. "I was thinking that having a visual guide of that plan might be helpful for you. It's been a tough few weeks, and if you each have a road map to peace, it might come in handy the next time you have a disagreement."

They both nodded. Elijah piped up and said he thought it should be comic-book style.

"That's a great idea!" I said. "I thought you both might want to make one with your own design and script so that it's customized for you."

FUTURE-FACING CONSEQUENCES

In chapter 9 we talk more in-depth about future-facing, empowering consequences. While I didn't use the word *consequence* in our conversation at the kitchen table, this is an example of a future-facing consequence. It equipped our boys with a tangible tool and reinforced skills to help them bring peace and respect to conflict in the future.

That afternoon I pulled out the art supplies, and they each set to work making their own road map to peace. True to his nature, Elijah created a comic strip with word bubbles and the most adorable drawings. Ezra's was more like a treasure map. And while their illustrations didn't include every detail of our family's PEACE Plan, they highlighted the steps to peacemaking and collaboration that were most important to them:

- Tell your side of the story.
- Listen to their side of the story.
- Find a solution that works for both.
- Ask "How can I make this right?"

Looking over their road maps to peace and problem-solving, I saw the bones of what we'd been teaching them for several years. They still had some details to fill in, but overall they did know how to navigate conflict with respect. And now they had something to help them remember how to do that. They looked back at their road maps multiple times that summer. They gave themselves *lots* of practice.

If you choose to follow the PEACE Plan, you may do a lot of guessing as you work to enact it during difficult moments, especially in the early years. After all, you're working to understand your child's perspective and needs, and they're working to understand the world! During this period of your child's life, they will need a lot of practice with the skills they will use for a lifetime. Just like they need training wheels and a steady hand to help them learn to ride a bike, they will need your trust-based support to learn obedience, collaboration, and conflict resolution. That isn't to say you should expect them to communicate, solve problems, mend relationships, or behave like adults. But be encouraged: This hard, sacred work early in your relationship with your child will establish a firm foundation of trust and influence that will impact your discipleship in the future. It's also a key tool to teach them to respect you and others.

Respect Is a Higher-Order Process

As parents, we tend to think of respect as being synonymous with obedience or listening. Teach kids to throw in a few cultural norms like "Yes, ma'am" and "No, sir," and we've got our playbook written! *If my kiddos are listening, obeying, and saying please and thank you, they're respecting me! And if they're not . . .*

We all know it's not nearly that simple. Yet in the nitty-gritty of long parenting days, it can be easy to make that leap. If trust-based obedience is rooted in honor and respect, we need to know how to cultivate an environment in which those attitudes will flourish.

Respect is, of course, an issue of the heart. But we can't forget that it's also a neurological process in the brain. Respect is a complex emotional and cognitive process that our children develop slowly over time! It is a higher-order response that requires critical thinking, memory, problem-solving, and complex judgment skills. These skills begin to develop during middle childhood, between the ages of five and twelve.[2] However, in stressful moments of conflict or fear, the executive part of the brain that leads to respect is inaccessible.

Recent research has also shown that respect isn't inherently given to those with authority or to those we fear. A 2020 study among an ethnically diverse group of children ages five to fifteen found that children as young as five are able to understand that respect is earned by how someone treats others:

> Across age, children frequently used prosocial themes
> when conceptualizing respect. This observation is
> inconsistent with Piaget's (1932/1965) position that

respect is authority-oriented and rooted in fear during early childhood. The finding instead suggests that *even at a young age, children are capable of appreciating and understanding that respect is reflected in the way individuals treat one another.* Thus, ethically relevant conceptions of respect emerge as early as 5 years of age.[3]

Children recognize the difference between genuine respect, which is rooted in how we treat others, and mere expressions of respect. I was reminded of this during a family dance party. As my kids and I listened and danced to a (kid-friendly) version of a catchy, lighthearted song about the paramount importance of kids listening to their mother, Ezra paid attention to the lyrics. When the song was over, he turned off the music player and pulled me down to his level. Looking me squarely in the face, he said in all seriousness, "That song is kind of rude to kids, you know."

I suppose in the moment I could have talked to him about music as art and how the song is actually a battle cry for working mothers. I could have brought up the concepts of sarcasm and satire, along with their place in art, music, story, and communication. But I just agreed with him. "Bud, I am so glad you're able to recognize disrespect. And more than that, I'm glad you're free to name it."

The findings from the 2020 study make an important point about the way we parent. As adults, we so closely associate respect from children with the way they behave—that is, whether they're listening to or obeying us. Yet we rarely associate our respect for children with our behavior toward them. Once we strive to earn their respect, not through fear and intimidation but through trust and love, everything changes.

It's easy to go with the mindset that children should respect their parents. But if that expectation is not balanced with a reasonable understanding of child development and a commitment to earn-ing our kids' respect, demanding it will be in vain. And any surface respect that children exhibit now will crumble once they are big enough and strong enough not to fear us anymore.

Disrespect Breeds Disrespect

When we as parents demand respect through harsh words or actions, it often gets us the result we want! But our kids' compli-ance, a by-product of the fear and stress response cycle activated by our anger, is a survival instinct, not genuine respect, trust, or love for us as the parent. It also creates a recurring cycle of disrespect.

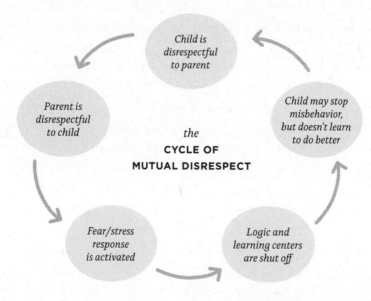

the
**CYCLE OF
MUTUAL DISRESPECT**

*Child is
disrespectful
to parent*

*Child may stop
misbehavior,
but doesn't learn
to do better*

*Logic and
learning centers
are shut off*

*Fear/stress
response
is activated*

*Parent is
disrespectful
to child*

The cycle of mutual disrespect is closely aligned with the nega-tive consequence/negative behavior cycle from chapter 4. As par-ents, we must use great wisdom and caution as we steward this knowledge of how our children's brains work and develop.

But just as importantly, we must remember that *our own brains* are an equal part of this equation; and adult brains respond to disrespect in the same way that children's brains do! Consider this scenario: Have you ever had a boss, coworker, or spouse treat you in a disrespectful way? Perhaps they micromanaged you, dismissed your thoughts and ideas, or interrupted or ignored you. Think about how your body *felt* in that moment. Remember that it takes less than a second for your self-preservation instincts to be triggered. From there, chemicals and hormones take over—your body is in pure survival mode. When you feel disrespected, your brain

SEE THE SIGNS OF DYSREGULATION

It is helpful to recognize that often what we perceive as disrespect is actually a sign of dysregulation. Back talk, inflexibility, defiance, and lashing out in anger are all indicators that a child's nervous system is not regulated. Some real or perceived threat has activated their fight, flight, freeze, or fawn response, and they're showing up to a fight!

There are usually warning signs leading up to an outburst of anger. As parents, we have the responsibility of learning to recognize those signs—in our children and in ourselves. Here are some common signs of dysregulation in our children:

- difficulty focusing
- shallow breathing
- hands in fists
- anxiousness
- crying or whining
- speaking in a snappy or snippy tone
- inability to sit still
- sensitivity to noise or touch
- using fewer words than they are capable of
- tight neck/shoulders/jaw
- low frustration tolerance
- excessive silliness
- big body movements: hitting, swinging, kicking

perceives that behavior as a threat, regardless of the intent. Even if you tried to rationalize the situation and let it roll off your back, that was probably difficult to do!

This exact same process happens in those heated moments of parenting. Whether it is a resolute toddler yelling, "No! I don't want to!" or an impulsive tween mouthing off over chores, it's inevitable that children will behave in ways we view as disrespectful. But even though we *know* our children are just *children*, our brains know no logic: Disrespect is disrespect, and disrespect is a threat. The stress response cycle is triggered, and it's off to the races—our bodies are now working solely from a mode meant to protect us and no one else. This is why it is imperative that we as parents learn how to regulate our own brains and bodies.

It's Time to Look Beneath

When my boys were young toddlers, I not-so-affectionately dubbed the late afternoon—when the boys played, squabbled, and fought in the living room while I was in the kitchen trying to make dinner—the "How're Hour." That's because I often wound up thinking, *How're we gonna make it until Daddy gets home?* One particularly challenging evening, I was on the verge of losing it. I texted David that I'd be walking out the door the moment he walked in because I needed a break. I needed room to breathe.

The moment he got home, I walked out the door, slamming it behind me. And I drove, mindlessly, with no real destination, my eyes blurry from crying so hard. Eventually I pulled into a scenic overlook about twenty-five miles from our house. I looked out over the thick piney woods of East Texas, screaming and crying until there was nothing left to come out.

As I watched the sky light up with evening majesty and then

slowly fade into a hazy dusk, I was frighteningly aware of how miserable I felt. I wasn't trying to manipulate anyone. I wasn't trying to be defiant. I wasn't trying to hurt my family. I just desperately wanted my needs to be seen and my voice to be heard. There was no malice in my motivations whatsoever; rather, I felt trapped in a never-ending cycle of being in an activated survival state.

Beneath my behavior were several factors, including

- unmet needs (hello, sleep deprivation)
- feeling invisible
- being disconnected from my support system
- postpartum anxiety
- being "hangry"

I had been so frustrated by my boys' disobedience and lack of cooperation; it felt personal, as if they were intentionally interrupting my agendas and *trying* to make life hard for us. But it was while sitting before the quiet stillness of an East Texas sunset that I realized: My children likely experienced many of the same under-the-surface struggles that I did. Their outward behavior, just like my own, was only the tip of the iceberg.

The Payoff of the PEACE Plan

As David and I came to understand more about how young children's brains develop and the need we all have for self-regulation and respect, I began to rethink the way I parented. The PEACE Plan was one result. And that long, hot summer I mentioned at the beginning of this chapter? It eventually came to an end, bringing with it cooler temperatures and the familiar rhythms of the school year. One Tuesday morning a few weeks into their first- and third-grade years, I was driving Ezra and Elijah to school. From the back seat I heard the beginning of conflict over a toy from the dollar store. Ezra had purchased the toy with his own money, and Elijah wanted to play with it.

The little handheld device looked remarkably like a video game, but when the control buttons were pressed, they pushed just enough air through the water beneath the screen to move little rings around. The goal was to get all the rings on some pegs.

Ezra didn't want to share his toy, which was extra frustrating because he wasn't even playing with it. He was finishing his breakfast and reading a book.

The road maps they'd created over the summer were at home, and I could tell from the tone of their voices that they needed a little coaching. "Hey, Ezra, I hear that you don't want to share that with Elijah. I'm wondering if you have a concern about something."

Ezra immediately responded in the affirmative. "Yeah! When I'm done eating I want to play with it, and my concern is he won't give it to me." That was a fair consideration, rooted in past experience.

"Oh, I see," I said. "I understand that because that's what happened yesterday. He didn't give it to you when you first asked for it." Because the goal is to get all the rings on the pegs, there is a clear "end" to the game, and because it's a game more based on chance than skill, it can take a while to finish.

Elijah piped up in his own defense. "*Yeah*, because I wasn't finished with my turn! *My* concern is I want to finish it!" When we tell you he has fire in his soul, we mean it. And he has no problem advocating for himself.

At this point I could have let them keep problem-solving on their own. They'd both stated their concerns, so they knew what the core problems were. But it was early in the day, and to be honest, I wasn't sure if it was going to go smoothly or not. Since I didn't want to be a distracted driver with kids fighting in the back seat, I offered a solution.

"Hey, Ezra, what do you think about this? What if Elijah plays with it now and when you're ready for your turn you can say, 'Hey, when you finish I'd like a turn.'"

He looked skeptical. "I could do that . . . but what if he doesn't give it to me?"

I silently acknowledged to myself that I had the same question. What *would* we do if Elijah didn't follow the plan? I didn't voice my concern, though, choosing to say instead, "That could happen. But this idea addresses his concern of being able to finish his turn with the game, right, Elijah?"

He nodded eagerly, fully on board. "Yeah! I just don't like having to stop before I'm done! Ezra, please can I play it?"

Ezra was still reluctant. I could tell that he wasn't ready to commit, and that if he said yes in this moment it would be more from a position of "whatever" than being truly invested in this solution. *That would be peacekeeping*, I thought. *We want to cultivate peacemaking.*

"Hey, bud, I can tell you're not sure about this plan," I said. "That's fair. I think this might be the kind of thing that we don't know if it will work until we practice. What do you think about just practicing?"

In the rearview mirror I saw him nod slowly. "Yeah, we can practice. But if he doesn't give it to me when he's done, then I'm putting it in my keeping box so he can't play with it." Ezra had drawn a clear boundary and communicated how he planned to enforce it.

Elijah agreed to the plan. Ezra handed over the water toy, and as we drove on in silence I turned on a podcast to help redirect our attention (which is especially helpful for Ezra). A few minutes later, I noticed Ezra playing with the toy.

"Whoa! I totally missed you asking Elijah for your turn! But it looks like the plan worked!"

With pride dripping from every word, Ezra said, "I *didn't* ask him for the toy! When I finished eating, he had just finished the game, so he gave it back to me and I didn't even have to ask!"

Elijah was grinning from ear to ear behind me because he had taken the plan to the next level, and he knew it!

"Wow! Elijah, thank you for paying attention and sticking to the plan! Ezra, thank you for sharing your toy with Elijah when you weren't playing with it. Our solution worked!"

They both did a little happy dance in the back seat, and my mind flashed back to that hot summer day and the road maps they'd made. We'd spent weeks referencing them, practicing bringing respect to conflict, and this morning our efforts had paid off.

Choosing to cultivate respect—even in the most difficult moments of parenting—is in no way the easy path. To be perfectly transparent with you, it often looks like messing up and modeling repentance and accountability. While our aim is to treat our children with unconditional respect, we also recognize that's an impossible standard. We as parents are prone to wander and miss the mark, just like they are. So if you read "unconditional respect" and thought to yourself, *That's it, I'm done with the book; I can never attain that goal,* you're in good company. We're all going to miss the mark sometimes—parents and children alike. But that doesn't mean we should change what we're aiming for. The moments when we fail are opportunities to point our children back to grace—and *our own need for a loving Savior who offers it to us daily.*

Learning to recognize that your child's personhood is more important than their behavior is a lifelong journey. But the final destination—a deep, respect-based relationship with your child—offers a beautiful view.

Reflection Questions

1. How does the concept of pausing before reacting resonate with you? Can you recall a recent situation when taking a moment to pause could have led to a more respectful interaction with your child? What strategies could you implement to incorporate the "Pause" step of the PEACE Plan into your parenting approach?

2. Reflect on a recent conflict you had with your child. What were the underlying emotions within you and your child in that situation? How might acknowledging these emotions have changed the dynamic? How can you better communicate your own emotions without placing responsibility for them on your child?

3. If you grew up in a home where respect for parents was demanded, not earned, what challenges do you see to internalizing the idea that respect starts with you as the parent? What steps can you take to prioritize this paradigm shift?

4. Review the PEACE Plan outlined in this chapter (see page 117). Choose one step that you find particularly challenging or intriguing. How can you practice incorporating this into your interactions with your child over the next week? What potential positive changes do you anticipate as a result?

Identifying the Root of Misbehavior

One Sunday afternoon as we were leaving church, Amanda asked, "What do you think about grabbing some lunch and running to Sam's Club instead of heading home?"

We live nearly an hour from the nearest small city, and our church is almost halfway there, so sometimes on Sundays we do the shopping that we can't do in our small town.

Even so, I (David) was skeptical. We had a lot on our plate, we'd just finished a crazy and hectic week, and another equally full week awaited us. And let's face it, when you take the whole family, there's really no such thing as a quick trip to town. I knew it might take all afternoon. I thought it would be more efficient to head home and eat lunch, and then I could head to the city and quickly do all the shopping, including at Sam's Club. I'd be home in time for supper. But the boys in the back seat had caught wind of the discussion and immediately began a campaign for us all to go into the city. Reluctantly I agreed.

For some reason we decided to eat at a sit-down restaurant. Then somebody mentioned how fun it would be to try the new indoor black-light mini-golf place. Our boys had an obvious agenda—have as much fun as possible. I also had a clear agenda—get the shopping done quickly so I could get home and start tackling my huge to-do list.

In a shocking twist, by the time we were a couple of stops into the shopping, everyone was grumpy. Frustration and disappointment were pulsating through the car, and I gritted my teeth as I heard whining and arguing from the back seat. Our family needed some peace.

So we took a pause from sharing the same space. I ran into the next store by myself. The boys played in a grassy area next to the parking lot. Amanda half scrolled Instagram, half kept an eye on the boys for a few minutes.

While I was in the store, I evaluated what was happening in me. I was super frustrated. I had wanted to make a quick shopping trip to get what we needed before facing another long week. Going out for lunch had already stretched the family budget. Paying for a round at the black-light mini-golf place would stretch it even thinner, plus then we would be in the city for so long that we would probably need to eat out for supper too. None of this was adding up for me.

I also acknowledged that our boys had had an equally long week that included being dragged to appointments and commitments outside their control. They had expectations for this trip because we had not given them any kind of clear plan for the afternoon. They filled in the blanks with what seemed good to them, and now there would be disappointment and frustration when those expectations weren't met.

When we all got back in the car, it was time to bring some peace into our family. As we sat in the parking lot, I said, "Guys, this day is not going as planned for any of us. There's a lot of frustration happening, and we all need some peace. Let's have a family meeting and follow our PEACE Plan."

So we did. We collectively took some deep breaths, releasing pent-up energy. We took turns communicating our emotions and needs and acknowledging how our actions and words impacted one another. Then we collaborated on a plan that worked for our whole family (and no, it didn't include going to black-light mini golf on that particular trip, but it did include putting that particular idea on our Family Date bucket list for the upcoming summer). And we made sure everyone was prepared for the last couple of stops on our shopping trip.

That emotional and mental reset took all of five minutes. It's a familiar plan that we've practiced often in our family. As our boys' verbal skills improved, it slowly became more natural to us. But even with years of practice, in the heat of the moment it isn't always our immediate response. It's something we have to choose to do.

Looking Deeper than the Behavior

At one time, we might have looked at our sons' pleas to go mini golfing as attempts at manipulation and their back-seat complaining as clear signs of disrespect. But we now recognize that a child's misbehavior may be their way of communicating hundreds or thousands of messages.

There are several popular catchphrases intended to help cultivate compassion for children when their behavior is challenging:

- "Kids do well if they can."
- "There's no such thing as a bad kid."

- "Children need to be reminded that they are good inside even when they act bad on the outside."
- "All behavior is communication."

Yet as Christian parents who desire to bring healthy spiritual formation to our children's lives, we can't just assume the constant goodness of our children. Yes, they may act poorly because they lack skills, have unmet emotional needs, are getting hungry or sick, need a nap, etc. The four statements above can be revealing and helpful reminders, but we also acknowledge that our inherent sin nature is another factor at play in behavioral situations. While we concluded that wrongdoing wasn't necessarily at the root of our sons' behavior on that Sunday shopping trip, there's no getting around the fact that sin is often a factor in the way all of us behave and express ourselves.

It can be helpful, then, to wrestle with and pray through the four common catchphrases alongside the following questions:

- How can we as parents tell if a child's behavior is a sign of an immature but developmentally normal brain or blatant, willful sin?
- Is an underdeveloped brain (and therefore immature behavior) part of God's original design, or is it the result of the Fall?
- How should I respond differently to my child's sins than to their immaturity?

These are good questions, and we fully celebrate the parents who are doing the beautiful work of daily working out their faith (Philippians 2:12) when they ask them. Yet these questions aren't simply and easily answered by referencing a Scripture verse or two. So let's dig in to what God says about sin and our children.

Handle with Care

When it comes to sin, some parents want to talk about it all the time. Anxious for their children to make a profession of faith as soon as possible, these parents primarily focus on teaching their children that they are sinners in need of a Savior. Every misbehavior is labeled as sin. Every kind of discipline includes a brief lecture on how the child has sinned against God. A feigned, forced "repentance" may often be required to restore relationships in the family. In many ways, the concept of sin has been weaponized as a behavior management tool.

Other parents never want to talk about sin. They assert that children are naturally innocent and good and will always want to do what is good. Rather than sin, misbehavior is just errant immaturity. It may be hurtful or harmful, but it needs only to be contained, not corrected, since children will grow into better behaviors. Nothing a child does is ever a sin or bad. In fact, the concept of sin is so dangerous that our children must be kept away from it.

Neither of these extremes accurately reflects how the Bible speaks about sin. Sin is real and terrible. No parent is free of it, and none of our children are either. It's also not the sum total of who we are, and it isn't our identity.

Our true identity

It's no accident that in the Bible, people aren't introduced as sinners. The first thing God reveals about humans is that we are made in His image. As we touched on earlier, every person—including every child—is made in the image of God. Being an image bearer is fundamental to our children's identities. It is a key message we communicate to our kids. Because humans bear the image of God, we are designed to be in relationship with Him and to take part in faithfully stewarding God's creation, and we can only fulfill our design in relationship with others. These are core messages every child needs to hear about themselves and their place in God's world.

Only after introducing humans in this way does the Bible introduce the reality of sin and its devastating effects. The awful consequences of sin form the dark backdrop for the rest of Scripture as God slowly unfolds His plan of redemption. Yet when Christ's redeeming work has had its full effect, humans will once again find themselves in a tree-lined garden, restored to unhindered relationship with God, worshiping in concert with others, and stewarding a new creation (Revelation 21-22). This is a reminder that the sin that comes so easily and seems so natural to us is not who we were designed to be. When it comes to our children, clearly laying down the message of who they are made to be sets the stage for us to clearly communicate how their sins and failures are a denial of God's good design for them.

Are we sinners?

This is not a book about sin. It's a book about parenting. But parenting as a Christian means acknowledging the reality of sin. Sin isn't something outside of us that trips us up occasionally. It's not the existence of money that makes a person greedy, the appearance of a woman that makes a man lust, or the position of authority that makes a person abusive. Those temptations have power over us only because of our sinful inward desires (see James 1:14-15). Put simply, we are always the source of our sin. We are the problem. Sin starts from within us and then shows up in our actions in the world around us. We sin because we willingly choose to.

Sin is also pervasive. There is no part of us that is untouched by our sin. Our thinking, emotions, reactions, desires, and virtually everything about us has been shaped by the reality of our sinful desires, our sinful actions, and the sinful desires and actions of others. When theologians speak of total depravity, this is what they mean. It's not that we are utterly depraved, but that the totality of who we are has been affected by sin.

When it comes to parenting, recognizing the pervasiveness of sin should cause us to be reflective about our own sin. It's easy to spot our children's wrongs. It's much harder to notice how we sin against them. We are all prone to think the best of ourselves. Instead of owning up to our mistakes and failures, we want to justify ourselves. We tell ourselves, *I wouldn't have yelled at them if they hadn't been behaving so badly.* Yet self-justification isn't the path of following Christ. Humility, recognizing our failures, and repenting of our sins—that is the path of a Jesus follower.

Acknowledging the reality of our own sin can also give us patience as we deal with other people's sins. When we anticipate that others will sin against us, we are more likely to respond with patience and grace rather than judgment and condemnation. If we're not perfect, then we shouldn't expect perfection from others—especially not from the young ones with slowly developing brains who are part of our families.

Why Does My Child Sin?

The real question is, why is everyone born with a sin nature? In answering this question, Romans 5:12 is a key verse:

> Just as sin entered the world through one man, and
> death through sin, in this way death spread to all people,
> because all sinned.

There's a lot to unpack in Romans 5 about sin, its consequences, and the way God responds to sin through Christ. Yet this one verse lays out the reality that because of Adam's sin back in Genesis 3, all people sin. There is no one who escapes this inevitable reality. Not you. Not me. Not our kids.

Different Christian denominations and theological traditions have slightly different ideas on exactly how sin is transmitted to every human, but they all agree that apart from the grace of God, all people are by nature sinners. This is fundamental to the Christian concept of humanity.[1]

This means that because our children are human, they were also born with sin natures. However, that does not necessarily mean our children are born sinning. What's the difference? The Westminster Confession of Faith describes it this way:

From this original corruption, whereby we are utterly
indisposed, disabled, and made opposite to all good,
and wholly inclined to all evil, do proceed all actual
transgressions. (6.4)[2]

This idea is not unique to one particular theological perspective, as can be seen in the Lutheran Formula of Concord:

The nature is nevertheless corrupted through original sin,
which is born in us by reason of the sinful seed, and is a
fountainhead of all other actual sins, as wicked thoughts,
words, and works. (I.11)

There's a difference between being born with a sin nature (corrupted) and engaging in sinful thoughts or actions (actual sin). Because they are born with a sin nature, all of our children inevitably will sin. But that does not necessarily mean they start engaging in actual transgressions as soon as they are able to express their will. Misunderstanding this difference has led some to describe young children as "vipers in diapers" who are little more than pint-sized criminals bent on the most heinous actions possible.[3] But is this how God speaks about children?

How Does the Bible Speak about Children?

In one of his letters, the apostle Paul writes, "When I was a child, I spoke like a child, I thought like a child, I reasoned like a child. When I became a man, I put aside childish things" (1 Corinthians 13:11). Let's be clear about what he is saying here— children don't speak like adults, think like adults, or reason like adults. This is such a basic insight that anyone who has spent time observing children would affirm it. But sometimes we as adults are quick to think that our children's reasoning and motivations are the same as ours. So we're glad that God enshrined in His Word a reminder that our children are not like us in all respects. Their immaturity and childishness are not character defects that need to be eliminated. Instead, they are part of God's design for how our children grow into their place in this world.

A recognition that children are not the same as adults persists throughout Scripture. Moses speaks about children as those "who don't yet know good from evil" (Deuteronomy 1:39). This hearkens back to the Garden of Eden before the Fall, when Adam and Eve didn't yet know good and evil. In one of his prophecies about the Messiah, the prophet Isaiah describes that as children grow, they learn "to reject what is bad and choose what is good" (Isaiah 7:15). Both passages describe the reality that children have not yet developed their ability to understand and make moral choices. While they slowly begin to grasp concepts like "good" and "bad," they initially do so in a very limited fashion. They don't yet truly understand the difference between good and evil and therefore don't have an internal capacity to choose good and reject evil.

In the early years, children tend to unquestioningly adopt the morality of their parents and their community. This is a vital time in their lives when we can lay deep moral foundations for their character. We can also squander those years by failing to model or teach a Jesus-centered life. Yet there inevitably comes a time when our sons or daughters understand good and evil beyond any immediate consequences but as the concepts relate to their Creator. At that point they will begin to make their own moral choices of rejecting the bad and choosing the good.

God makes clear that children are not to be held guilty for the sins of their parents, nor are parents guilty for the sins of their children (Deuteronomy 24:16; Ezekiel 18:20). This is brought into focus dramatically when the young people of Israel were not held guilty for the nation's refusal to enter the Promised Land after ten of the twelve spies gave a bad report. After telling the Israelites that almost everyone twenty and older would die in the wilderness, God promises that "I will bring your children whom you said would become plunder into the land you rejected, and they will enjoy it" (Numbers 14:31). The adults were held fully accountable for their sin and faithlessness (Numbers 14:33-34), while their children ultimately obtained the promise that had been given to their parents (Joshua 1:2-3).

Given all this, it's not surprising that Jeremiah refers to children as "innocent" (Jeremiah 19:4). Those who do not know the difference between good and evil are rightly called innocent. The prophet Ahijah also declares that God regards King Jeroboam's young son as having "something good toward the LORD God of Israel" (1 Kings 14:13, NKJV). Was Jeroboam good? Clearly not. He had led Israel into idolatry. Jeroboam and all his other sons were held accountable for their sinful and destructive leadership of the nation. But his young son was not. Why did God find something good in him? The only difference between him and his older brothers that we're told about was that he did not yet know the difference between good and evil. Therefore he had not yet rejected the good and chosen evil. He was still innocent.[4]

The language of innocence may sound jarring to us, especially those of us who see that the Bible clearly teaches that sin is universal and pervasive. Yet this language is consistent with a God whose judgments about human moral responsibility are connected to human moral capability. Our children may be corrupted by their sin nature, but they are innocent of the knowledge of it.

None of this undermines or diminishes the reality that our children are each born with a sin nature. But it calls into question our ability to accurately determine when our children have knowingly and willfully sinned. If the Bible acknowledges that children think in childish ways and lack the ability to fully understand good and evil, how are we to determine which actions are caused by immaturity and which ones are caused by sinful desire? The Bible doesn't answer that question with the clarity and specificity we might prefer.

Instead, it challenges us to seek wisdom, and in seeking wisdom, we learn to ask the questions that give us direction instead of leaving us feeling stuck. And, ultimately, as followers of Jesus, we can let go of the need to have all the "right" answers because our trust is in the Way, the Truth, and the Life, not in having the right answers.

The Bible Is Not a Behavior Modification Handbook

Despite what some pastors and Christian authors might tell you, the Bible is not a book about you and what you should do. It is about God, what He has already done, and what He is persistently inviting you to join Him in.

This is true for us as parents who are faithfully seeking to live out our faith as disciple makers of tiny humans with beautiful souls. And it is true for our children as well. Simply put, God is not merely trying to manage our behavior, nor should we as parents find our primary purpose in managing our children's behavior.

Yes, there are times when you must step in and immediately correct your children. Situations related to safety are obviously such circumstances, and there are others as well. Thankfully, those moments become fewer and further between as our children grow and mature. But in many instances, immediate behavior modification isn't terribly productive toward long-term, or Jesus-centered, goals.

Parents have many good goals for their children, but what is our chief goal as Christian parents? For our children to know, trust, and experience God in such a way that their hearts are turned to Him.

And heart change? That's the work of grace.

Do you show contempt for the riches of his kindness,
forbearance and patience, not realizing that God's
kindness is intended to lead you to repentance?
ROMANS 2:4, NIV

Here's the beautiful truth that sustains us as we live with faith and hope for our children: When our hearts are changed by grace, we are motivated to do good works because of the grace we've been given. When we are captivated by Christ and transformed by His Spirit, we will grow in fruitfulness and faithfulness!

The way of Christ's Kingdom is this: Transformed hearts result in changed behavior. But changed behavior cannot produce transformed hearts. Just because we instill good habits in our children, teaching them to practice good manners and to apologize and share, we cannot expect that they will have the mind of Christ and a love for Him.

The only thing that will change a child's heart is the power and presence of the Holy Spirit. So to punish them for their struggle or their sin accomplishes no spiritual good. At best, all efforts to modify their behavior in a "godly" direction will create scrupulously ethical sinners. At worst, it could be the means of driving them from the Kingdom of Christ.

We want our children to take sin seriously, knowing that it is an eternally serious matter. As a result, we are tempted to think we can teach the seriousness of sin through punishment. But our children will never learn the infinite seriousness of sin by being punished for a few of them. They will only truly understand sin when they gaze on the One who is worthy of all earthly and heavenly praise because He suffered and died on the cross for our sins. This is the primary way that God teaches us about sin—through His own self-sacrifice. There is no punishment we can mete out that will teach our children about sin more effectively than the dazzling display of grace found at Calvary.

Acknowledging that heart change in our children's lives is the sole work of God should feel like chains breaking and sweet freedom to our souls! But it should not leave us without any expectations or boundaries for our children. While our ultimate goal isn't behavior modification, we are called to lead, guide, instruct, and nurture our children toward wisdom, maturity, and discernment. Conversations about actions and consequences as well as the ways in which we can sin against others and against God are a normal part of childhood in the home of Jesus followers. Done at an age-appropriate level, these discussions intentionally prepare our children's hearts for the convicting work of the Holy Spirit.

Responding to Sin or Struggle

How should we respond to our children's sin? There is plenty in the Bible about what Christians should do when others sin. Space does not permit us to review it all here. But it seems worth highlighting the first time in Scripture a father responds to his children's sin, which we find in Genesis 3:8-24. As we watch God respond to Adam and Eve right after their very first sin, we discover some ideas of how we might respond to our children's sin:

- God moves toward them. Adam and Eve have broken the relationship, but God still seeks them out. When our children do something wrong, we don't isolate them in hopes that they'll "learn their lesson." Instead, we move into the relationship— physically, emotionally, or both. As the adult, we will set the tone that leads either to reconciliation or to shame.

- God calls Adam and Eve to understand what they have done. His questions aren't designed to elicit information— He already knows! Rather, He is guiding them toward self-awareness and understanding of their actions. As parents, we can fall into a trap of asking too many questions in an attempt to determine who exactly started the fight or to get a confession from the guilty party. Of course, parents aren't all-knowing, but we can focus more of our attention on helping the child move toward understanding what went wrong and how they can start fixing it.

- God does not save Adam and Eve from all the consequences of their sin. They had to live with what they did. Natural consequences haven't been fun since the beginning. It can be hard to let our children experience the consequences of their choices, but it's much better for them to learn hard lessons when the stakes are small than to learn those lessons later in life when the stakes are much greater.

- God does not curse Adam and Eve. He curses the serpent and He curses the ground, but He doesn't curse those who are made in His image. Pray that God would set a guard over your mouth so that you would speak carefully to your children, especially when you're angry or frustrated. Let your mouth bless and not curse your children.

- God does not shame Adam and Eve, even though they experience shame. Instead, He covers their disgrace. Our kids will experience shame in life. We can't prevent that. But we don't need to humiliate them, much less mock or ridicule their failures. Let our grace cover their shame.

- God puts in place boundaries that prevent Adam and Eve from suffering even worse future consequences. He sends them away from the Garden so they will never be able to eat from the tree of life, which would leave them in their sinful state permanently. Logical consequences are sometimes exactly what our kids need, just like they need boundaries that give them assurance that we are looking out for them.

The Lord's response to Adam and Eve reminds us that our goal when our children sin is not to blame, shame, or demean. Instead, it is to fulfill what the apostle Paul directly commanded Christians:

Brothers and sisters, if someone is caught in a sin, you who live by the Spirit should restore that person gently. But watch yourselves, or you also may be tempted. Carry each other's burdens, and in this way you will fulfill the law of Christ.

GALATIANS 6:1-2, NIV

As parents, our goal when our children sin is simple—restoration. Whether they've sinned against us or against someone else, restoration and reconciliation is always our intent. In fact, whether we think our children's misbehavior was caused by their immaturity or by their sinful inclinations, our response won't actually change. We'll connect and correct, clarify the path to reconciliation, and teach them how to show up better next time. We can do all of that with gentleness, not harshness—just as our heavenly Father does for us.

Reflection Questions

1. How would considering the root of misbehavior change the way you interact with your child in difficult moments?

2. When reflecting on your approach to parenting, do you find yourself often dwelling on the sin nature of your children, or do you avoid the issue of sin altogether? What would a healthy, balanced view of sin in relation to misbehavior look like for your family?

3. As you consider the way God reached out to Adam and Eve following the Fall (see page 148), what action do you most want to emulate when connecting with a misbehaving child?

4. Recall an instance from your childhood when you remember choosing to sin. How would you have wanted your parents to respond to you? What would it have looked like for you to have received mercy and grace in that situation?

9

Discipline as Discipleship

One Wednesday night, we arrived home late from church, where we'd just spent an hour teaching forty or so children. As we unloaded the car, Ezra and Elijah got into a heated and intense argument. As the situation escalated and they erupted, Elijah's brand-new but already well-loved shirt was accidentally torn.

Perhaps it was an ironic coincidence (or maybe just God's sense of humor), but our lesson that night had been about being peacemakers. When we asked the kids if they had any stories about a time they hadn't gotten along with a sibling or a friend at school, we opened a floodgate of raised hands and fast-paced storytelling. One by one, most of the kiddos, craving to be heard, told a story from their life.

Our own two sons had sat in on the lesson, though none of it was new to them. By this point, they were fairly familiar with our PEACE Plan, and they even helped us act out a few scenarios that night.

Though we weren't there when the argument started, we both bore witness to the shirt getting torn. It truly was an accident, leaving both boys in tears. Because it was well past bedtime, we resolved as a family to come back to the ripped shirt in the morning. We worked to help the boys calm down and get ready for bed. Then we had a parent meeting to figure out how we were going to address this in the morning.

You may be thinking, *There has to be some form of discipline for your boys. They need to learn to be accountable for their actions during the argument.* What should discipline look like in this situation? We hear you loud and clear, so we want to invite you on a journey that reimagines discipline less as punishment and more as discipleship.

Punishment for the Past

When many of us hear the word *discipline*, we immediately assume it to mean "punishment." This isn't a surprise—our society teaches us over and over that accountability for wrongdoing must be retributive and punitive; that is, we have to pay for our wrong behavior through an experience of pain.

Take driving, for example. If you drive recklessly, you get a ticket. The hope is that by having to pay the ticket (financial pain), you'll be motivated not to speed again. It's easy to apply this idea to parenting. If your children speak disrespectfully, common parenting advice would be to punish them with a time-out. They go to their room by themselves and "think about what they've done." The hope is that by being physically isolated in this way (and experiencing the emotional pain that this separation brings), they will think twice about repeating the wrong action in the future.

They'll remember what happened last time, want to avoid the punishment, and decide against speaking disrespectfully again.

Let's be frank: When it comes to modifying, managing, and changing behaviors, punishments do often work in the short term. Time-outs have been found to improve behavior, as have related consequences.[1]

However, when we remember that God designed our bodies to respond to fear by going into a fight, flight, freeze, or fawn response, which minimizes the capacity to learn so we can protect ourselves or survive the perceived threat, we can see potential flaws in this approach. The short-term win often comes with a long-term loss. Only when the brain perceives safety, love, and security can a person be receptive to new information, experiences, and challenges. Research consistently shows that corporal punishment, both in the home and in the classroom, is often linked with poor outcomes later in life.[2] It is only if the punishment (time-out, loss of privilege) is accompanied by verbal correction and conversation that its long-term impact becomes more neutral.[3]

Further, children, especially those who are young, often won't make the negative association we want them to see between their behavior and our response. Rather than remembering the misbehavior that got them in trouble, they will focus on the punishment and whether they felt it was fair or just. Mac Bledsoe, longtime coach and teacher, author of *Parenting with Dignity*, and father of star NFL quarterback Drew Bledsoe, offers a revealing insight:

> When a parent resorts to punishment, parent and child pay attention to the punishment, its fairness, and whether it has been enforced or followed. The child stops thinking about the *decision process* in his mind that brought about the negative behavior—and doesn't think at all about what he might do differently.[4]

Knowing that our bodies and spirits respond to punishment in such a counterproductive manner will transform our approach as parents.

Discipline as Training

Admittedly, moving away from punishment is a hard mindset shift to make, especially as Christians. We may have been taught punishment-affirming Scripture by respected pastors or leaders as far back as childhood. For example, Hebrews 12 seems pretty conclusive when it says, "For the Lord disciplines the one he loves and punishes every son he receives" (verse 6) and "No discipline seems enjoyable at the time, but painful" (verse 11). There it is: An open-and-shut case for painful punishment as necessary in Christian parenting. Right?

Again, the context of Scripture is key to truly understanding its meaning. When we take in all of Hebrews 12 and its preceding context, we see that the author intends to paint a very different picture. Throughout the book, the author of Hebrews has been exhorting his audience to steadfastly pursue faith in Christ, urging them not to shrink back from following Him (Hebrews 10:26-39) but instead to follow the examples of the faithful saints of the Old Testament who remained true no matter what difficulties they faced (Hebrews 11). He opens chapter 12 with a beautiful encouragement to "run with endurance the race that lies before us" (verse 1). We can do that only if we keep our focus on Jesus; otherwise we will grow weary and give up in the face of hostility, persecution, and suffering (verses 2-4).

In our world, suffering is always seen as a bad thing. If you suffer, it's because you've done something wrong. The book of Job, however, is a long repudiation of that erroneous theology.

Jesus also directly rejects such thinking (see John 9:3). Here in Hebrews 12, the author again calls us to reject the idea that if God loves us and we follow Him, we will never suffer.

Instead, the author of Hebrews explains that suffering is not a sign of God's rejection but proof that we are indeed His children. He also reminds us that our suffering is being used by God and has a purpose in our lives.[5] To substantiate his point, the author quotes from Proverbs 3:11-12:

> My son, do not take the Lord's discipline lightly
> or lose heart when you are reproved by him,
> for the Lord disciplines the one he loves
> and punishes every son he receives.
>
> HEBREWS 12:5-6

The word translated "punishes" in the last line is important. We've seen people try to pretend it's just not there or that it doesn't mean what it pretty obviously means. We don't think we should handle the Word of God so lightly. There is really no way around the fact that the word translated as "punishes" literally means "to whip." Yet when we looked more closely at this passage, we made two fascinating discoveries about this word.

When we go back and read Proverbs 3:12, we find that it says, "for the LORD disciplines the one he loves, just as a father disciplines the son in whom he delights." Hold on a second. Where is the word *punish* (*whip*)? Did someone mistranslate Proverbs? No. Your English translation of Proverbs is accurate. In the original Hebrew, Proverbs 3:12 talks about discipline but not punishment or whipping. It was only when Proverbs was translated from Hebrew into Greek (a translation known as the Septuagint) that the word for *punishment* was used. It is this Greek translation of the Old Testament that is being quoted in Hebrews 12 (which was also written in Greek). So that's how the word *whip/punish* came into this context.[6]

But then take note of what the author of Hebrews does with the idea of punish/whip: He does absolutely nothing with it. His entire argument centers on showing that suffering is discipline that enables faithfulness. The concept of punishment is irrelevant to what he is saying, so he ignores it.[7] The laser-like focus on discipline in the book of Hebrews makes sense if you remember that the goal of the author is to encourage his audience to "run with endurance the race that lies before us" (Hebrews 12:1). As he closes out his argument about suffering as discipline, he returns to the athletic theme by encouraging his readers to "strengthen your tired hands and weakened knees, and make straight paths for your feet, so that what is lame may not be dislocated but healed instead" (Hebrews 12:12-13). The discipline God gives to His children is not about punishing them for their failures but about training them for faithfulness.[8]

When you read Hebrews 12:1-13 with the understanding that it's about how to successfully run the race of faith, discipline takes on a very different meaning.[9] Professional athletes are some of the most disciplined people you will ever meet. They spend years training their bodies for peak performance. Only the most committed make it to the top of their sport. They are disciplined, not through punishment, but through careful and committed training, practice, study, and coaching. Their skills and abilities are developed through years of hard work.

What if we approach the training of our children in the same way? Like athletes, their skills, choices, and behavior take many years and much practice to develop. They need coaching, guidance, and equipping so that they can truly succeed and thrive. With this in mind, our goal in discipline shifts away from punishment and focuses instead on teaching and training—or, to put it in Christian terms, *discipling*—our children so they will be motivated and equipped to do the right thing because it is the right thing, not because they fear retribution.

While punishment focuses on past behavior, discipline focuses on future behavior. It prioritizes preparing and equipping a child to show up or do differently next time. It doesn't ignore what has happened or permissively go along with misbehavior as if it were okay. But it isn't preoccupied with past unwanted behavior. Future-focused discipline allows us to evaluate our children as whole beings, taking into account their physical, emotional, and sensory needs; their personalities; and their development. That enables us to create a robust and holistic approach to empowering them for the future.

Discipline as Teaching

It can be easy for parents to focus solely on behavior and how to change it. In fact, in all our years of mentoring and coaching parents, every single person who has reached out to us has asked how to stop a specific behavior. And to be fair, even within the pages of this book we've offered ideas and plans for responding to *behaviors* with peace and purpose.

We've been there—when we began this journey, we were asking the same questions you are. Then we examined Paul's instructions in Ephesians 6:1-3 for children to obey their parents. As we noted, Ephesians 6:4 and Colossians 3:21 provide the only direct commands to parents in the New Testament about *how* they are to raise their children within the Kingdom ethic that Jesus inaugurated and the early church lived out. The order presented to parents in Ephesians and Colossians—first to be aware of a child's emotional state, then to teach and train them in the Lord—was radical in the first century. Yet again, we see how modern neuroscience is catching up to God's divinely inspired blueprint!

When we consider Paul's letters to the early church, we realize that we may need to shift our parenting priorities: Not one word is written to parents about controlling or managing their children's behavior. Instead, what do we see? *Do not anger them, do not provoke them, and do not discourage them.* This should tell us that our children's hearts, not their behavior, are what truly matters.

We cannot overstate the importance of this paradigm shift. You do not nurture children's hearts by managing their behavior. You nurture their hearts through love, trust, and safety. If you're trying to correct your children's hearts, but the root of the problem is developmental, you risk hardening their hearts! This doesn't mean we just ignore their behavior. Thankfully, Paul doesn't leave us with only a general encouragement to be aware of our kids' emotions. He follows that with the directive to "bring them up in the training and instruction of the Lord" (Ephesians 6:4).

As we discussed in chapter 6, we can't take this verse without a strong contextual grounding. Many Christian authors have, with understandable fervor, taken this command to mean that we are to raise our children *in Scripture.* And we don't disagree with that! However, in Paul's letter to the church at Ephesus, he tells parents specifically to raise their children in the training and instruction of *the Lord.* The difference here is important: When Paul composed this letter, there was no New Testament. So if God had intended the meaning of Paul's words to be an encouragement to raise our children in the Scripture, he would have been exclusively referring to the Hebrew Bible (the Old Testament).

This distinction is an interesting one to ponder because the church at Ephesus is believed to have been made up predominantly of Gentile converts. Their level of familiarity with the Torah and Prophets is unknown, though Paul's reference to verses from Exodus and Deuteronomy in Ephesians 6:2-3 may be a hint that they had some knowledge of them. Regardless, this brings to mind an interesting question: Does *in the Lord* refer to Scripture or to the Lord Jesus Christ?

Of course we agree that raising children with the help of God's Scripture is integral. But Paul's wording here can't be overlooked. When he encourages raising children "in the Lord," he opens the door to shame-free, trust-based parenting with grace as the foundation. As Christian parents, we are to raise our children in the instruction and training of Jesus. In His way.

And what is His way? We see in the Gospels that, in His interactions with people, Jesus persistently and radically responds to aggression, disobedience, impulsiveness, pride, rivalry, violence, and lack of trust with grace, kindness, compassion, and sometimes with firmness. He confronts sin without adding shame. He corrects and rebukes with clarity but not coercion. While we may not see in Jesus an example of what to do when our toddler dumps a plate of food on the floor, we do see Him kindly meeting needs, patiently correcting, and boldly inviting those around Him to walk in His footsteps. He models for them God's best for humanity as He lives out the Kingdom of Heaven amid the messiness of earth.

It was this way of living, modeled after Christ and His teaching, that revolutionized the early church and turned the world upside down in a history-shaking transformation that has never been seen before or since. It is as radical today as it was then. In Jesus we see that more effective than the promise of reward or the threat of punishment is the call to discipleship.

Reconciliation and Restoration

Our boys were still young toddlers when we were convicted to view discipline more as discipleship and less as punishment. In theory, this was great. In practicality, we often felt lost. Cue the late-night Internet searches for "how to help a toddler not hit" and "how to respond to toddler tantrums." Finding resources specifically for Christian parents was a little trickier—especially for early childhood. Rather than piling on shame, punishment, or condemnation and inadvertently teaching our children to focus on their own feelings about their behavior, we wanted to use the example of Jesus to guide our discipline. We wanted to teach accountability through reconciliation and restoration.

When we commit to this type of accountability, we are not committing to a life without consequences! The opposite, in fact, is true. Disciplining as a peacemaker embraces natural consequences as beautiful, God-designed learning opportunities, and prepares children with skills and practices to help them show up differently in the future.

And let's be honest, that can be tough! As parents, we often view consequences in one of two ways: Either we don't want our children to experience the consequences of their choices (so we try to step in and shield them) or we feel like the natural consequences aren't enough to teach the lesson (so we impose additional punishment).

But this is not what we see modeled in Scripture.

Let's return to the parable of the good, good Father (Luke 15:11-32). In chapter 4, we looked at how the father graciously gives the Prodigal Son the demanded inheritance. The son chooses to travel afar, waste all he has been given, and steadily debase himself until he is a starving pig herder. Finally, he comes to his senses. Only now does he recognize the graciousness of his father, a man who cares not just for his family but also for the lowliest of his servants.

The son decides to return home and beg for forgiveness. He hopes he can be a slave. It will be a life of permanent shame, mockery, and service to what had once been his family, but it's better than starving.

When he arrives home, this plan immediately falls apart. Instead of the father making his son grovel and beg or even ask permission to come inside the house, the father runs to him and begins to hug and kiss him. The father cuts off the son's well-rehearsed speech asking to be treated like a servant. Instead, the father immediately treats him like a treasured and trusted son. He tells his servants, "Quick! Bring out the best robe and put it on him; put a ring on his finger and sandals on his feet. Then bring the fattened calf and slaughter it, and let's celebrate with a feast, because this son of mine was dead and is alive again; he was lost and is found!" (Luke 15:22-24). It's not the robe, sandals, or

JESUS' DISCIPLESHIP AS A MODEL FOR OUR DISCIPLINE

- *He lived as a constant example:* "I have given you an example, that you also should do just as I have done for you" (John 13:15).

- *He developed a close relationship with His disciples:* "I have called you friends, because I have made known to you everything I have heard from my Father" (John 15:15).

- *He taught in ways His disciples could understand:* Jesus used parables to explain important ideas (Matthew 13) and used many everyday events as examples to make His points clear (Luke 21:1-4).

- *He met His disciples' needs before or during teaching moments:* By providing them with needed food, sleep, bodily healing, and physical safety, Jesus showed care for His disciples.

- *He empathized with His followers in their emotions, even when their feelings were misplaced:* He met Mary and Martha in their grief and didn't try to correct their accusations (John 11).

- *When confronting or correcting sin, He didn't condemn but offered a path to restoration:* By forgiving the woman caught in adultery, Jesus made clear that sin rarely needs immediate condemnation. Instead, people need transformative grace that leads to restoration (John 8:1-11).

- *He gave the disciples opportunities to practice what they were learning:* From sending them out in pairs to proclaim His message (Mark 6:7-13) to intervening when their attempts to emulate Him failed (Matthew 14:28-31; Mark 9:14-29), Jesus regularly let His disciples practice their faith.

even the feast he gives his son that is most surprising. All of those could be excused as the excesses of an excited father who believed he would never see his son again. They represent grace given where only shame is due, but the father is a man of otherworldly graciousness. The father literally covers his son's shame with a robe and then obliterates it with celebration.

The shocking part, however, is the ring. This is not just a decorative piece of ornamentation; this is a signet ring. It gives the son authority to act on behalf of the father—to buy, sell, and borrow.[10] If there is anyone who should not have this kind of authority, it is this son. His track record of financial irresponsibility is long. He has in no way shown himself worthy of this trust, despite having finally made one good decision in his life. Giving the ring is a huge risk for the father. He gives his son the power to destroy even more than he already has.

Here's the interesting thing about the father in the parable: He doesn't impose any punishments or consequences on his son. He knows that the son has already suffered the consequences of his foolishness. The father doesn't add to them.

This is radical grace. Society tells us that if we give too much grace, our children will turn into hooligans who don't know the difference between right and wrong. It tells us that we'd better keep our love tempered if we want to provide good moral training for our children. Yet God's love is anything but temperate. Some might even call it reckless. But through that love, God forms the moral character of His children.

"C" Is for Consequence

How do we apply this beautiful display of grace and wisdom to our own parenting today? After all, this is a parable about a father with grown children, and it would be a misapplication to argue that we must be endlessly permissive and have no boundaries in our relationships with our children. Yet similar to the father in the parable, we can allow natural consequences to refine and shape a child's internal motivations. This often yields less obvious immediate results than traditional punishment, and it may seem like our children are "getting away with" repeated negative behaviors. But when we allow consequences to teach our children's hearts, they become internally motivated to pursue the right actions because they see the benefit or goodness for themselves. No longer are they choosing good behavior out of fear of what Mom or Dad will do to them; they're choosing the better action because they understand for themselves why it is superior.

Natural consequences

When we commit to parenting with peace and purpose, we take our cue from the good, good father, learning to identify and lean into natural consequences, which are the expected, unavoidable result of a choice or behavior. They require no interference from an adult and rarely require explanation or lectures.

The week our dog got hold of Elijah's brand-new toy that he'd left out overnight was the week our younger son started valuing our nightly habit of resetting (tidying) the living room before supper. That one natural impact of his choice not to pick up his toys taught him more than any lecture or punishment ever would have. It was so impactful that he also began taking the initiative to pick up his brother's toys when he noticed they'd been forgotten.

Natural consequences are powerful teachers, though not always immediately. Because we've been so programmed to expect instant results in almost every area of life, it can be quite a challenge for parents to recognize how powerful natural consequences can be!

EXAMPLES

> When your young child hurts another child, the natural consequence may be that the hurt child doesn't want to play with the aggressor.
>
> If your child leaves a toy outside, it may get rained on and ruined.
>
> When your child doesn't want to wear their coat, they may get too cold at the park.
>
> If your child won't share one of their toys, that friend may not let them play with one of theirs.

The wonderful thing about natural consequences is that they also provide positive reinforcement! Positive natural consequences help children recognize the beneficial impact their choices have—for themselves and others.

EXAMPLES

> When your child is kind to another child, they may be invited to that child's home to play.
>
> When your child helps put away toys, they have a clean play space in the morning.
>
> When your child puts their shoes in the closet, they know where to find them the next time they need them.
>
> When your child takes turns, everyone gets a chance to play with the fun toy.

Logical consequences

Of course, we as parents sometimes need to enforce a boundary or hold a limit. Is there a way to do that without resorting to threats or punitive consequences? Yes! We like to reframe logical consequences as "loving limits" held with gentle firmness. They can be helpful tools for keeping children, animals, and belongings safe.

They are not used punitively; instead, they are used proactively to avoid painful natural consequences when a child is dysregulated, which is an act of grace and kindness.

Gentle Consequences	Punitive Consequences
• I can tell you want to throw! It's not safe to throw in the house; let's go outside where you can throw as much as you want to.	• If you don't stop throwing in the house, I *will throw* the toy, and I'll throw it *away*!
• You're really sad to leave the park. I understand. I'll hold you while we walk to the car.	• If you don't go to the car, we won't come back to the park!
• You're overwhelmed with all the toys to put away. Let's think of which toys we can take a break from for a few weeks so that pick-up time isn't so overwhelming.	• If you don't pick up these toys, they are going in the trash!

In general, logical consequences are primarily used with younger children who have not yet developed impulse control (about ages one through seven). These consequences are a tool to help enforce boundaries and hold limits. We do that based on the child's developmental abilities; therefore, when a logical consequence, or loving limit, is needed, it must make sense to the child and be reasonable for their age, cognitive development, personality, and temperament. When we think of logical consequences within the context of holding boundaries or limits, we see that they are directly related to the child's choices and actions rather than being arbitrary and punitive reactions. They are a connected progression or outcome of what is already in motion, and thus should be somewhat "expected" by the child.

We cannot overstate this: It is very easy for logical consequences to actually be punishments in disguise. Yes, there are times when logical consequences are needed, and in those cases, be aware of your tone of voice and nonverbal cues, such as your facial expressions, posture, body movements, and gestures. These all signal to your child whether or not the consequences you impose are punitive.

EXAMPLES

When young toddlers are hurting each other, they must be separated.

If your child will not hold your hand in the parking lot, they need to ride in the shopping cart or be carried.

If your kindergartner can't or won't stop throwing a toy inside, they can go outside (or the toy can be temporarily put away if going outside isn't an option).

When your child throws food on the floor, they help clean up the mess.

"HOW CAN I MAKE THIS RIGHT?"

Teaching very small children about accountability and reconciliation may seem like a daunting task. One simple way to start is by helping them understand that an apology isn't simply saying, "I'm sorry." Restoring broken relationships means actively seeking to make things right.

We taught our boys that a full, heartfelt apology comes in their own time, when they are ready to say it and mean it, rather than according to our schedule (we don't want them to learn to say things they don't mean just for the sake of peacekeeping), and includes the question "How can I make it better?" or "How can I make it right?"

We also taught them that sometimes forgiveness and restoration are effortless. Grace is extended and the relationship moves forward. But other times, rebuilding trust takes time and tangible effort. When we noticed tension between them as they got older (around grade school age), we started asking, "Is there something to be made right, or is this something to let go of?"

Imposed consequences

When parents employ imposed consequences (which easily can be thinly veiled "nicer" punishments), the child's focus turns to the consequence and its impact on them, rather than on their behavior and its impact on others. Instead of learning the important lesson that their choices influence and impact others, they become focused on how the consequence influences and impacts them.

EXAMPLES

When your child doesn't put away their laundry and you take away screen time, your child focuses on the injustice against them rather than on learning how putting away their laundry benefits them and others.

When siblings fight and are told they can't go to a friend's party on the weekend, they focus on the arbitrary consequence rather than learning conflict resolution skills.

When your children won't do their homework and are given extra chores, they will focus on their frustration with these tasks rather than learning how to manage their priorities and time well.

Imposed consequences are very common in mainstream parenting. But we've found they are almost always either based in fear and a need to control a child's behavior or choices, or they are utilized because the parent doesn't know what else to do. When we shift our mindset to trust-based, peacemaking parenting, we seek to guide, not control, a child's choices and behavior. We also recognize how ineffective and inefficient imposed consequences really are, which makes it easier to take them off the table.

You may be thinking, *Take imposed consequences completely off the table? Are you kidding me?* And we get it; it is so radically outside what we as individuals and as a culture are used to that it is hard to imagine what the results would be. As you recalibrate your parenting to a Jesus-centered grace and accountability mindset, we encourage you not to get hung up in all-or-nothing thinking. Rather, shift your thinking to not relying on imposed consequences to change behavior. The goal is for your child to trust your wisdom, guidance, and love, not to fear the consequences you hand down.

Future-facing consequences

One of the weaknesses of negative consequences is their inability to teach children how to act differently or do better in similar situations in the future. And one of the struggles parents have when letting go of their dependence on negative consequences is knowing how to help their children not get stuck in habits of misbehavior. This is where future-facing consequences empower both parents and children.

Future-facing consequences can take several forms, many of which may not feel very much like discipline. For example, young children who act impulsively (remember, this is by God's good design!) will benefit from playing games that strengthen their ability to inhibit urges and impulses, such as Simon Says; Red Light, Green Light; and Follow the Leader. These classic childhood games play an invaluable role in building the impulse control "muscle" in children!

As with any skill and ability, repetition, failure, learning from mistakes, and trying again are all critical parts of the learning process. Role-playing nurtures children's learning and skill-building, so inviting your children to act out various scenarios is another great future-facing consequence.

We shared an example in chapter 7 of giving our boys the task of creating their own PEACE Plans as a future-facing consequence when their sibling conflict was out of control. You may find it helpful to think of it like this: Rather than punishing a child for how they showed up *this* time, evaluate how you want them to show up *next* time, as well as the wisdom and skills they'll need to practice. Then create opportunities for your child to practice what you want them to learn.

Nonretributive Accountability

We've found that when it comes to an authoritative parenting style like we've been describing, a common misunderstanding is that grace and accountability are mutually exclusive. Nothing could be further from the truth. When Ezra tore Elijah's shirt that Wednesday night, we were given a very real opportunity to teach both boys about accountability. Even though it was an accident, Ezra's actions had natural consequences: Elijah's shirt was torn, and he was sad about it!

The next morning, we had a quick family meeting. We circled up with our boys on our living room rug, with cozy blankets wrapped around us and silent prayers swirling within us. After recapping the events of the night before, we reminded them that, accident or not, the shirt was torn. We then invited them to work together to find a way to make this right.

At ages six and seven, their ideas ranged from doing absolutely nothing to Ezra replacing the shirt with his own money. You can probably guess who submitted each of those solutions. They also discussed sharing a similar but not identical shirt (a benefit of them being so close in age), or the brother at fault learning how to mend.

As a family, we decided that Ezra learning to mend the shirt was the ideal path forward, as it would not only repair the torn garment but also put real action toward repairing the relationship between the two boys. Together, David and Ezra sat at the sewing machine and stitched a crooked but adequate new seam.[11]

This is but one example of nonretributive accountability. This is what future-facing, restorative discipline looks like in action. This is parenting with peace and purpose, where grace and accountability are sacredly intertwined in Jesus-centered discipleship.

Because there is such a wide range of age-appropriate behaviors that are nonetheless typically considered inappropriate or unacceptable—such as hitting and biting in toddlers, lying in preschoolers, and attitude and back talk from older children—we as parents will frequently find ourselves seeking wisdom and discernment as we guide our children. Their maturation in body and behavior spans many years, and it can sometimes feel disheartening when we witness slow progress in persistent challenges with our children. During such moments, it's important to remember that seeking outside perspectives can be valuable. Experienced parents, trusted mentors, dedicated parent coaches, or trained professionals can provide fresh insights and strategies to help us navigate these challenges effectively. Remember: Seeking help is a sign of strength and a commitment to providing the best guidance and care for our children.

Reflection Questions

1. What does accountability mean to you as a parent? How can you teach your children about accountability with gentleness and grace, as opposed to pain and punishment?

2. When you have suffered in your own life—whether now or in the past—does a part of you believe that this difficulty is a sign of God's rejection or disapproval? How can

you remind yourself (and your children) of the truth of people's belovedness, even in suffering?

3. Think of an area in your child's life in which you'd like them to grow or improve. How does changing your perspective of your role as a parent to that of a trainer or coach alter the way you approach and tend to that area in their lives?

4. The topic of discipline and consequences in parenting can be filled with tension and misunderstanding. What are some Bible verses (either from this chapter or elsewhere in Scripture) that can serve as anchors as you endeavor to align yourself with God's view?

10

What about the Rod?

I (Amanda) remember the first time I spanked our older son. Ezra was fifteen months old, I was six months pregnant, and he wouldn't stop wiggling as I tried to change his diaper. His squirming and rolling on the changing table was more than I could handle in my sleep-deprived, swollen-belly state. He was not cooperating, and I didn't know what to do. Without thinking, I smacked his chunky little thigh. Of course he immediately stopped squirming. For half a second he looked at me in shock, and then he started crying. I cried, too, mostly from frustration with him, but also from frustration with myself.

"I'm so sorry. I'm so sorry," I whispered to him as I held him close. I already knew I didn't want to be heavy-handed when it came to spanking, and it felt incredibly disempowering to recognize that

I lacked the patience and skills to work with a protesting toddler over a diaper change. But it wasn't until hours later that I realized the full impact of hitting my child.

That evening Ezra was playing on our living room floor. I heard him start to fuss and walked over to check on him. As I leaned down toward him, for the first time ever he pulled away—literally recoiling from me. I could see the fear in his eyes, and instantly I knew that I had broken his trust in me when I spanked him on the changing table hours earlier.

I have got to find better ways to discipline him. I can't do this too many times or he won't trust me! I thought.

As I lay in bed later that night, I googled "toddler discipline without spanking." A trove of resources appeared at my fingertips, and I clicked "Add to cart" on several books that sounded promising. I realized I was starting on a new parenting journey as I resolved not to use spanking unless absolutely necessary. (It would be a little less than a year before I took spanking completely off the table.) But little did I know that I was embarking on a new spiritual journey as well. I had been warned, "Spare the rod and spoil the child," and I wholeheartedly believed that spanking was biblical. Yet the more I read about the effects of spanking on developing brains, and the more I learned about respectful, peaceful, and authoritative parenting, the harder it was to reconcile in my heart that Scripture could allow, much less endorse, spanking.

Thankfully, God's Spirit is kind and gentle with us. And His wisdom is peace-loving and full of mercy (James 3:17). Together David and I began studying ancient Jewish culture, the history of Bible translation, and a few words in the Hebrew language that have shaped entire generations of Christians. What we discovered completely reshaped our parenting paradigm.

Spare the Rod?

"Spare the rod and spoil the child" is popularly believed to be straight from the Bible. It's frequently touted as definitive proof that God wants us to strike our kids when they misbehave. There's one problem: It's not in the Bible. It's right up there with sayings like, "God will never give you more than you can handle" and "The Lord helps those who help themselves." They sound a little bit like the Bible, but they're not actually in Scripture.

Isn't the idea rooted in Scripture, though? Aren't there verses that tell us to spank children? Usually what most people have in mind are a few verses in Proverbs that talk about a "rod."

The rod verses

There are four passages in Proverbs that are frequently used to justify spanking:

> The one who will not use the rod hates his son,
> but the one who loves him disciplines him diligently.
> PROVERBS 13:24

> Foolishness is bound to the heart of a youth;
> a rod of discipline will separate it from him.
> PROVERBS 22:15

> Don't withhold discipline from a youth;
> if you punish him with a rod, he will not die.
> Punish him with a rod,
> and you will rescue his life from Sheol.
> PROVERBS 23:13-14

A rod of correction imparts wisdom,
but a youth left to himself
is a disgrace to his mother.
PROVERBS 29:15

To put these in context, other passages in Proverbs also talk about the rod, whether directly or indirectly:

Wisdom is found on the lips of the discerning,
but a rod is for the back of the one who lacks sense.
PROVERBS 10:13

The proud speech of a fool brings a rod
     of discipline,
but the lips of the wise protect them.
PROVERBS 14:3

Judgments are prepared for mockers,
and beatings for the backs of fools.
PROVERBS 19:29

Lashes and wounds purge away evil,
and beatings cleanse the innermost parts.
PROVERBS 20:30

A whip for the horse, a bridle for the donkey,
and a rod for the backs of fools.
PROVERBS 26:3

At first glance, it would appear that we have conclusive evidence that God commands His followers to spank their children. But what if there's more to consider?

What is Proverbs really talking about?

A closer look at the book of Proverbs as a whole will provide helpful context for understanding how we are to interpret and apply these verses.

Proverbs are wisdom sayings that generally are not taken as literal commands. How do we know? Because we don't insist that a glutton take a knife to their throat to curb their appetite (Proverbs 23:2). How many times have pastors advised the husband in a troubled marriage to move up to the roof (Proverbs 21:9) or go live in the wilderness (Proverbs 21:19)? Trying to treat proverbs as literal directives will make the book nonsensical because many of the proverbs offer conflicting advice (see Proverbs 26:4-5). It's a book meant to impart wisdom, and we have to be wise in applying it to specific situations.

Yet age-old questions still linger: Even if the Bible doesn't command parents to spank their children, doesn't it still recommend it? If Solomon says spanking is a good idea, who are we to argue differently? Doesn't that mean Christian parents should spank their kids? Isn't God telling us that this is the wise way to parent?

These are good questions that often are asked by well-meaning, deeply devoted Christian parents. But there's one question that usually goes unasked: How did we decide that these proverbs are talking about spanking? If we're going to use these verses to support spanking children, shouldn't we make sure that Solomon is actually talking about this practice? It takes some investigating to determine what these proverbs meant in Solomon's day, but it's so worth it. Let's dive in.

Who is on the wrong end of the rod?

Let's look at who Proverbs mentions the rod being used on. If you compare a few different Bible translations, you'll get slightly different answers. For example, compare Proverbs 22:15, first in the English Standard Version and then in the Christian Standard Bible:

> Folly is bound up in the heart of a child,
>   but the rod of discipline drives it far from him.

> Foolishness is bound to the heart of a youth;
>   a rod of discipline will separate it from him.

In English, *child* and *youth* aren't the same word. When you visit a church and ask to see the children's ministry area, no one ever takes you to the youth room. We use these words to describe different ages of young people. So the question of whether Solomon is talking about using a rod on a child or on a youth is an important one to consider. If the rod verses are about children, then they would seem to support spanking. If they're about youth, then we're talking about something else. So how do we decide which one is correct?

Digging into a little Hebrew

Since these proverbs are from the Old Testament, our first goal is to find the Hebrew word translated *child* (ESV) and *youth* (CSB) to determine its meaning. Thanks to the vast number of free online Bible study tools available, it's pretty easy for anyone to discover that the Hebrew word is *na'ar*. Looking it up in a Hebrew dictionary, we find this definition: "boy, lad, youth, servant, attendant."[1] A number of Hebrew words are used in the Old Testament to refer to babies, children, young men, and young women at various stages of life. The one used most frequently is *na'ar*, and it is the term used in the "rod" verses in Proverbs, so it's helpful to look more closely at this word.[2]

Dictionaries are great, but they only give us possible meanings.

They don't tell us what a word means in a particular sentence. To know that, we have to figure out how a word is used. This is why we do something called a word study. Put simply, we need to look up all the times *na'ar* is used in Scripture.

Who is a **na'ar**?

Ferreting out what exactly *na'ar* means requires real commitment. It shows up about 240 times in the Hebrew Bible. Yet in the vast majority of cases, *na'ar* is used in one of two ways. First, *na'ar* is used for the period of life when a young man is able to work and live independently of his family but has not yet married and established his own family. In ancient Israel, this age roughly coincided with what we now call the teenage years.[3] This was a time when young males were growing into manhood, but also a season when biblical authors saw them as particularly susceptible to being foolish and straying into sin.

Second, the Hebrew Bible often uses *na'ar* to refer to a servant. It's not the only Hebrew word for servant or slave, and many times the *na'ar* seems to be someone in a position of responsibility in the household. We often find this servant managing other people or engaging in conversation with the head of the family. It seems to indicate a position of trust well above menial labor. Unlike the use of *na'ar* for a young man, the *na'ar* as servant doesn't seem to describe any particular age. It's used for young boys who fetch arrows and men old enough to be grandfathers.[4]

Can a **na'ar** be a young boy?

In all likelihood, the *na'ar* in Proverbs is either a young man or a servant. Yet there are some rarer uses of *na'ar* in the Old Testament that don't fit neatly into those two categories. There are a handful of times when *na'ar* is used for a young boy. That seems relevant to this discussion, so let's look at these uses more closely.

The first use of *na'ar* as a very young boy refers to the infant Moses when his mother placed him in a basket and sent him floating down the Nile (Exodus 2:6). Samson was called a *na'ar* by an angel while still in his mother's womb. The angel declared to his parents that Samson was already a Nazirite, and therefore his mother had to follow certain restrictions while her body nourished his (Judges 13:3-8). Another instance refers to Samuel when he was a toddler being prepared to spend a lifetime serving in the Tabernacle (1 Samuel 1:22-28). Ichabod was referred to as a *na'ar* when he was born. His father, Phineas, and grandfather, the priest Eli, had just died that day, and his mother was dying after giving birth to him (1 Samuel 4:19-22). The final very young *na'ar* is King David's first baby with Bathsheba, who is called *na'ar* when he lay dying as part of God's judgment on David's sin (2 Samuel 12:15-16).

There's a common thread that ties each very young *na'ar* together: Every one of them was removed from his father's authority, whether through the death of the boy or the father, the boy physically being away from his father, or the boy being called by God to a life of divine service. In all these cases, the word *na'ar* is used to denote the reality that the boy is independent of his father, notably at a far younger age than one would expect.[5]

One final note: Proverbs 13:24 mentions using a rod on a son. The Hebrew word used here for son (*ben*) does not have any specific age connotations, whereas *na'ar* typically does (young men). So one might really try to stretch and say that this verse advocates spanking young boys. Yet this interpretation would make this verse unique in the Bible. It also understands this verse in a way contrary to the whole of Proverbs, which clearly has young men in mind throughout. Put simply, using this verse to justify spanking young children isn't a plausible interpretation given its context.

What Does This All Mean?

To sum up what we've found in this word study, let's look at the three possibilities for who the *na'ar* is in the "rod" verses in Proverbs:

- He is an older son who is not quite a man.
- He is a servant of some kind.
- He is a young boy who is not under his father's authority.

How should we decide among these alternatives? By reading Proverbs, of course! First, we know that the father-son relationship is a major theme of Proverbs: "Listen, my son, to your father's instruction" (Proverbs 1:8). So that makes "servant" a less likely possibility. We also learn that the entire book is meant to teach "knowledge and discretion" to a *na'ar* (Proverbs 1:4). While there certainly are some Proverbs that are applicable to young children, many of them are really applicable only in the teenage years and beyond. That makes the older son a more likely possibility. Solomon also describes the *na'ar* as being susceptible to the wiles of the seductive woman (Proverbs 7:7-10). Clearly in that instance the *na'ar* cannot be a young boy who has yet to reach puberty. This type of obvious usage, along with the fact that the Bible consistently presents a young *na'ar* as outside his father's control, makes it highly unlikely that these "rod" passages refer to a young boy under his father's authority.

Looking at the Hebrew word *na'ar* makes it pretty clear that Solomon is not talking about spanking children. He's talking about using the rod on young men, youth, and teenagers. If we're looking for biblical support for spanking toddlers or preschoolers, the "rod" verses don't offer any.

What Is the Rod?

If Solomon isn't explicitly in favor of spanking children, he is in favor of corporal punishment in general, right? Maybe. We need to figure out what Solomon was referring to when he used the word translated as a "rod."

The Hebrew word for rod (*shebet*) is a broad word that can have a variety of meanings. At its most basic level, a rod is a wooden stick. Often it has been shaped or purposed so that it is a shepherd's staff, a walking stick, a club, or a scepter. It is also used in more metaphorical ways for the wielding of authority (by one who holds the scepter) or for a clan or tribe of people.[6]

How will we decide how Solomon understands the rod in Proverbs? Again, by looking at the context. It's pretty clear that he expects the rod will be used to deliver a beating on the backs of fools (Proverbs 10:13; 26:3). It's an instrument of corporal punishment used to deliver what in modern terms we would describe as a "caning."[7] We have no compelling reason to interpret it differently in the proverbs concerning youth.

The rod used for corporal punishment is mentioned a few times in the Hebrew Bible. Limitations are placed on its use so that those being beaten won't be degraded in the eyes of others (Deuteronomy 25:1-3). People are instructed to use it with caution because it could injure, maim, or even kill a person (Exodus 21:20-21). The rod of the Hebrew Bible is a serious instrument for delivering harsh beatings, so Proverbs anticipates that blows from a rod will leave wounds and marks. In fact, these visible wounds are taken as signs that evil has been cleansed from the person (Proverbs 20:30).

Proverbs also applies the rod exclusively to the back of a person

(Proverbs 10:13; 19:29; 26:3). This is consistent with instructions found in the Law of Moses that a person being beaten should lie down while the punishment is administered (Deuteronomy 25:2). Nowhere does the Bible advocate for or even mention the rod or any other similar implement of corporal punishment being applied to the buttocks of a person. It was always and exclusively applied to the back.[8]

If this description of the rod sounds worse than spanking, that's because it is! The ancient world was harsh, and corporal punishment was used for a variety of offenses. Ancient Israel was notable among its neighbors for placing restrictions on this form of punishment, but adult freedmen could be punished with up to forty blows with a rod (Deuteronomy 25:3), and slaves could be subjected to even harsher punishments, so long as they survived (Exodus 21:20-21). That's not to mention the death penalty, which is the punishment for numerous offenses in the Law of Moses.[9]

The rod was not intended to be used as the first means of training. Proverbs expects escalating forms of discipline, including encouraging proper behavior, pointing out misbehavior, informing of consequences, exhorting to righteousness, rebuking bad behavior, beating with a rod, and finally capital punishment.[10] Knowing this helps us make sense of Proverbs 23:13-14, in which the rod is presented as saving a youth from hell or death. In a context where a continually disobedient older son could be handed over to the community and stoned to death (Deuteronomy 21:18-21), a beating with a rod could be the means of saving his life. Essentially, in that context, given a choice between someday soon handing over a teenage son to be executed or beating him now, the wise father should choose to beat him. That's a hard choice, but it makes sense in its ancient context.

TAKE CARE WITH TERMINOLOGY

We sometimes speak with parents whose views on spanking are partly based on misunderstandings of terms. For instance, some people want to interpret the rod in Proverbs as a shepherd's staff used to guide, not hit, the sheep. This uses Psalm 23:4 to determine the meaning of *rod* in Proverbs. Unfortunately, this interpretation is a type of lexical fallacy. The meaning of a word is not simply determined by picking the meaning we like best in the dictionary. The context shapes what is the most likely meaning. Nothing in Proverbs suggests that the rod is being discussed in the context of shepherding, but there's a lot to indicate that it is being used in the context of corporal punishment.

Another error some people make is due to a poor translation of the Hebrew word *Sheol* in Proverbs 23:14. While a few Bible versions render this as "hell," it really referred to death and the place of the dead. It was not the same as the place of eternal condemnation. Yet this poor English translation has led some people to believe that using the rod will save their children from hell. Not only is that based on a bad translation, it's also bad theology. Saying that the rod can save anyone is a denial of the finished work of Christ and salvation by grace through faith.

The Big Picture

Here's the simple fact: In the rod verses, Solomon is talking about beating teenagers or young men so they might learn not to be foolish. Their original audience would not have understood these passages to be about spanking children. We can only interpret the passages that way if we ignore both the actual words inspired by the Holy Spirit and the original historical context.

Yet let's be absolutely clear: These passages do not justify beating a teenager or young man today. The entire world of corporal punishment present in Solomon's day has disappeared. The town square no longer has a whipping post or gallows. Recall that just two hundred years ago Christians were using their Bibles to argue that slavery was good, husbands should beat their wives to keep them in line, and criminals must be whipped. You would be hard-pressed to find a Christian making such arguments today. Why? Did the Bible change? No. Christians got far more serious about reading Scripture faithfully and applying it with a Christ-centered lens. We outlawed slavery, wife-beating, and cruel punishments not because there was a specific Bible verse that told us to do that, but because following the path laid out for us in the teaching of Jesus and the apostles led us to do that. Yet in some communities today there remains a vestige of that entire system of punishment—the spanking of children. Every other part was gone long before most of us were born.

In the modern Western world, the use of the rod as described in Proverbs is considered abusive. We know of no Christian pastor or parenting author who advocates for the beating of teenagers. Even among the most ardent pro-spanking advocates, we have yet to find any that actually take these verses literally. Instead, the rod verses are assumed to be an endorsement of corporal punishment in general. The thinking seems to be that since Proverbs includes examples of corporal punishment that are much harsher than anything a loving parent might do to their children today, then God is clearly fine with less severe forms of corporal punishment like spanking.

The trouble is that the modern practice of spanking is being done on a person of a different age, with a different implement, on a different part of the body, with a different severity, and with different physical results than the examples we read in Scripture. The only connection between the rod of Proverbs and spanking of children is that someone is getting hit. Everything else is different.

FALSE EQUIVALENCY: SOLOMON'S ROD VERSES VERSUS MODERN SPANKING

	Understanding in Solomon's Time	Misunderstanding Today
Age	Youth, young men (teenagers)	Infants to grade-schoolers
Implement	Wooden stick capable of maiming or killing a man	Hand, spoon, paddle, dowel
Location	Back	Buttocks
Results	Visible wounds are expected	Visible wounds are abusive

We don't get to shape and mold Scripture into the words we want. The Bible cannot mean something now that has no foundation in what it meant when it was written. This is a cardinal principle of biblical interpretation. Otherwise, any of us can twist Scripture into supporting anything. We really cannot use the passages on the rod in Proverbs to support spanking children. If God wanted to encourage or endorse the spanking of children, He certainly could have, but He didn't. Let's not assume that He did.

Even though God's Word never says anything in favor of spanking, it also never says anything directly in opposition to it. It is one of the many aspects of life that God did not choose to address directly. Instead, we are called to use relevant principles found in God's Word to help us learn the mind of Christ on particular questions. We have already covered many of those relevant principles in this book. None of them point toward a need for spanking, and many of them orient us away from using such punishments on our children. We are also called to use the wisdom from human powers of observation to help us discern the best path for parenting. What God's Word and God's world reveal about children and parenting are perfectly consistent, as we discussed in chapter 3. Given that, we now turn to the knowledge gleaned from human observation.

What Does Science Say?

Through a multitude of studies conducted over many decades and in a variety of cultures, there has yet to be one that finds any positive benefit linked to spanking. Most of the data available indicates a persistent correlation between spanking and negative long-term outcomes for children.

Let's take a look at three studies that highlight what science has been able to learn about spanking and its effects.

The Gershoff/Grogan-Kaylor study

In 2016, a study released by child development and family science experts from the University of Texas and the University of Michigan found spanking to be closely associated with antisocial, aggressive behavior; depression and anxiety; and an increased risk of thirteen detrimental outcomes.[11]

The meta-analysis examined more than fifty years of research involving more than 160,000 children, and child development experts quickly touted it as the most comprehensive analysis on the topic. What sets Gershoff and Grogan-Kaylor's work apart is that they evaluated the effects of spanking, slapping, and hitting children when administered *without the use of objects* and found that spanking is still associated with negative outcomes.

This study, which makes a distinction between spanking and child abuse, led the American Academy of Pediatrics in 2018 to officially condemn spanking as a disciplinary tool:

The AAP recommends that adults caring for children use
healthy forms of discipline, such as positive reinforcement
of appropriate behaviors, setting limits, redirecting,
and setting future expectations. The AAP recommends
that parents do not use spanking, hitting, slapping,
threatening, insulting, humiliating, or shaming.[12]

While this study ultimately led to the AAP's strong stance against
corporal punishment, researchers, child development experts, and
child advocates have been speaking out against corporal punishment of children for decades.

The "Gray Matter" study

In 2009, a study found that in some situations, spanking children
actually reduces the development of gray matter in their brains.
Gray matter is the brain tissue behind all mental functions, including language, reasoning, learning, and intelligence—all the things
children are developing throughout childhood. The study examined the effects of using an object, such as a paddle or belt, to
spank the child only when it "was used on occasion for the purpose of disciplining a child, provided it did not extend beyond
the buttocks, was not conducted out of anger, and did not result
in injury." The authors reiterated throughout the study that this
form of corporal punishment occurred "specifically for discipline,
with parents in emotional control, and not striking out in anger."[13]

The "Elevated Neural Response to Threat" study

In May 2021, a study published in *Child Development* explained
how researchers had examined the brains of children who were
and were not spanked to see how each child's brain responded to
perceived environmental threats. Their findings showed that children who were spanked exhibited greater responses to perceived

threat, suggesting that spanking can alter children's brain functions in ways similar to more severe forms of maltreatment.[14]

In an interview, the study's lead author, Jorge Cuartas, pointed out that "spanking elicits a similar response in children's brains to more threatening experiences like sexual abuse. 'You see the same reactions in the brain,' Cuartas explains. 'Those consequences potentially affect the brain in areas often engaged in emotional regulation and threat detection, so that children can respond quickly to threats in the environment.'"[15]

Research consistently reveals that spanking is not only ineffective in teaching children to behave correctly or do what's right, but it also brings significant risk of short-term and long-term negative outcomes. This emerging evidence explains why the overwhelming majority of child development experts and researchers in the fields of neurology, psychology, and social services advocate against spanking.

Rethinking the Way We Discipline

On the international front, spanking and other forms of physical discipline have increasingly been understood to be human rights violations. "In 1989, the United Nations (UN) Convention on the Rights of the Child . . . called on all member states to ban corporal punishment of children and to institute educational programs on positive discipline."[16] At that time, four countries around the world had banned corporal punishment; to date, more than sixty countries have banned or outlawed spanking.

Notably, Israel banned corporal punishment of children in 2000. Dr. Yitzhak Kadman, former executive director of the National Council for the Child, said this decision "finally recognized the right of children not to be exposed to violence of any kind, even when those who use violence make excuses for it, saying it is 'educational' or 'punitive.'"[17] This strong stance against corporal punishment by a country that still observes much of the Old Testament Law should give Christians pause with how we interpret the Hebrew Bible on this issue.

Throughout this book we have demonstrated that punishing a child for what they have done in the past provides them with no better understanding of how to behave or interact differently in the future. This applies to us as parents, as well. Simply laying out the lack of evidence in Scripture and the nearly universally accepted negative impact of spanking fails to empower and equip parents to be peacemakers. In fact, without providing ample parenting tools and strategies to replace spanking, presenting this information alone could be highly disempowering for many parents.

As you move forward with this awareness, a better understanding of child development, and a clearer vision of how Jesus' teaching and ethics inform and shape Christian parenting, we hope the tools and strategies in this book empower you with a fresh perspective on discipling, nurturing, mentoring, and guiding your child as they mature physically, emotionally, and spiritually.

Reflection Questions

1. Think back to the last time you spanked a child or saw a child getting spanked. What could have been done differently prior to that moment? What strategies do you need in interacting with your child during difficult situations to help you before you get to the point of wanting to spank them?

2. What messages might we be communicating to a child when we spank them? Are those messages beneficial to them? Do they help them find and follow Jesus?

3. What do you find most surprising about the meaning and context of the "rod" verses? How do they impact your view of spanking?

11

Fostering Wisdom

For Ezra's sixth birthday, we bought him a scooter. Perhaps it wasn't the best decision on our part because we live in the country and have a dirt driveway. That meant he had nowhere to ride but the concrete carport. He headed out there every chance he got as he learned how to scoot, mostly in circles.

Later that summer we were working on the yard and I (Amanda) had to make a run to the garden store near closing time. As I headed to the car, I noticed Ezra's scooter lying in the driveway a few feet behind my car. I could have moved it myself (and truly wouldn't have minded doing that), but Ezra was playing nearby, and I wanted to give him the opportunity to take ownership of his scooter.

Instead of saying, "Ezra, come move your scooter!" I walked over to him and said, "Hey, I want to show you something. Will you come with me?" He was excited to join me, and we headed toward the car. When we got to the scooter, I said, "I'm about to head to town to get some things for the yard."

"Oh, do I have to go with you?" he asked.

I could tell he wasn't tracking with me yet. "I'm going to make this trip by myself," I said, "but I wonder if you see anything that needs to be done before I leave." I intentionally left the question open-ended because I wanted to see if he would pick up on what I was getting at.

He didn't take the bait. "Do you need to take a shower?" he asked. And of course, I laughed because, to be fair, I was literally a hot mess after working outside.

I went on to explain that I wasn't actually done working in the yard, so I would be heading to town just the way I was—hot, dirty, and tired. "But I noticed your scooter here behind my car," I said, pointing to it.

That's when I could see in his eyes that the proverbial light bulb had gone off. But he didn't jump into action, so I asked another question. "Hey, bud, what do you think would have happened if I hadn't seen the scooter and just started backing up?"

His eyes got really big and serious. He gasped in little-person horror and said, "It would have gotten smashed."

"I think so too. What do you think we should do to make sure that doesn't happen?"

He jumped into action before he started to answer. "I'll move it over here!" he said enthusiastically, steering the little scooter up against the wall of our carport.

Now, he was only six, and the scooter did show up behind the car a few more times before he developed the habit of putting it away when he was done with it. But those curious questions invited him on a journey of discovery and fostered thinking through decisions, actions, and consequences far better than just telling him to put away his scooter. He was on the path of developing wisdom in taking care of his possessions.

The Wrong Goal

As we've explored in this book, many parenting experts value obedience much more than wisdom, especially in the early years. The most critical thing for parents to teach their children, they say, is to obey. This will teach them what it means to obey God, guarantee the child's safety, ensure family harmony, and just make life easier on the parents.

Yet we also know that what many people count as obedience is really just temporary compliance by their child—the parent manages to compel their child's body to do what they want it to do. But forced compliance doesn't lead to trust-based obedience, genuine honor, or life-giving wisdom.

Consider what it would be like to have perfectly compliant children. You issue a command and they immediately follow it. Every time. Without fail. They never complain, whine, or object. Especially on the tough days, it sounds like a dream come true. The problem is that it's exactly that: a dream. It isn't at all realistic; yet such behavior is sometimes held up as the ideal for children. In certain Christian circles, obedience is so revered that it is, in all practicality, an idol.

And while completely compliant children may sound fabulous during the toddler and preschool years, what would happen as they continue through life? The compliant boy goes along with the class bully and helps him harass other kids. The compliant young woman gives in when her boyfriend pushes past her sexual boundaries. The compliant young man goes along with his friends when they suggest drinking or trying drugs. The compliant woman tolerates an abusive marriage because she's never learned how to stand up for herself.

Compliance is a counterproductive goal if we desire to prepare our children for the real world. Obedience is only as good as the person who's being obeyed. When a child is two and the parent—the center of their entire world—is someone with only their child's best interests at heart, compliance as a means of obedience might work. But what about when the child is twelve and that parent—rightly—is no longer the center of their world, no longer the only voice they listen to? The child now regularly interacts with people who don't have their best interests in mind. If they've been trained to comply with everyone who seems to have authority, they will be easy targets for manipulators and narcissists.

What our children really need is wisdom.

If you're reading these pages while in the throes of toddlerhood or the preschool years, we understand if you feel some tension and struggle with this idea. The stage of life you're in is a challenging time in parenting—you are constantly balancing laying a foundation for your children's future independence with meeting their very real dependency in the moment! And we also know that it is unreasonable to expect your toddler to have and exercise wisdom. Wisdom is learned. And while we all wish our children would gain wisdom immediately, that isn't how it works.

Imagine for a moment that your small child has entered their teenage years. Their baby-powder smell has been replaced with body odor, and their night-light has been exchanged for the glow of their phone. They're spreading their wings and learning to fly, possibly catching odd jobs here and there as they look for something more permanent. They have their own money to spend and their own dreams to chase. And their sphere of influence has expanded to include their peers. More and more they venture out into the world without you, hopping in the car with a friend after church to get slushes at Sonic or with a classmate after school to study for finals. You're still a significant influence in their life, but your presence is no longer constant. They're straddling independence and dependence like they used to straddle a swinging gate, sometimes nearly as dangerously!

The question we want you to ask is, when your child arrives at the crossroads of independence and dependence, do you want them to begin experimenting with decision-making, or do you want them to have had years of practice? Do you want them to depend on outside voices and external motivation—doing something simply because someone told them to—or do you want them to turn inward, tuning their hearts to the ultimate Source of wisdom and using their own wise discernment?

The Heart of the Matter

Throughout the Old Testament—but especially in the Prophets—we see time and again that, to God, simply following His rules is insufficient. What is of more importance to Him is the heart. God promises that He will give His people a new covenant and replace their hearts of stone with living hearts of flesh (Jeremiah 31:31-34; Ezekiel 36:26-27; see also Hebrews 8:7-12). By turning their hearts toward God, they will find joy in following Him. It will change them from the inside out.

The Old Testament closes with a promise that things will change in the future. These are the last words God inspired before going quiet for four centuries:

> Look, I am going to send you the prophet Elijah before
> the great and terrible day of the LORD comes. And he will
> turn the hearts of fathers to their children and the hearts
> of children to their fathers. Otherwise, I will come and
> strike the land with a curse.
>
> MALACHI 4:5-6

What is this hope that Elijah will one day herald? It's a hope that the hearts of parents and children will be transformed so they turn toward one another. It's a hope for parenting that is not about external compliance but heart transformation.

But those words aren't only how the Old Testament closes; they are also how Luke opens his Gospel. When speaking to the priest Zechariah, an angel from God makes clear that this hope has been fulfilled, starting with John the Baptist:

> He will go on before the Lord, in the spirit and power of Elijah, to turn the hearts of the parents to their children and the disobedient to the wisdom of the righteous—to make ready a people prepared for the Lord.
>
> LUKE 1:17, NIV

John the Baptist preaches a message of repentance and the imminent arrival of the Kingdom of Heaven. He prepares the way for the Messiah and announces His arrival. This is all part of the grand narrative of the Bible, but what does it have to do with parenting?

When we think about the messianic hope that is fulfilled in Jesus, we tend to narrow in on the eternal salvation provided through Jesus' death, burial, and resurrection. But the good news of Jesus cannot be confined to a hope for a heavenly future. When John the Baptist announces and Jesus then inaugurates a new Kingdom, everything—including parenting—is forever changed. As followers of Jesus, we parent as Christians, as people whose hearts have been transformed by Jesus.

But the angel isn't done. Notice that, after quoting Malachi, he goes on to mention those who are disobedient. The answer to disobedience? Surprisingly, it's not obedience! According to Luke 1:17, the antidote for disobedience is righteous wisdom.

The goal is not to turn disobedient children into perfectly obedient children. The Pharisees already had a plan to ensure external compliance. No, the real goal is so much greater—we parent to turn our children toward the wisdom of righteousness.

Biblical Wisdom

I (David) remember being a young teenager and trying to fit in with my friends by using cusswords. One day in a frustrating situation, I let fly with a few choice words. Except this time I wasn't just with my friends. My dad was there too. For context, my dad is a straight arrow. I've never heard him use even the mildest obscenity. On top of that, my dad is a university professor who literally lectures for a living. But he didn't lecture me or even correct me in front of my friends.

Days later we were driving (and I was a captive audience) when my dad asked me, "How well do you think you represented Jesus the other day when you said those words?" Behind that question were years of teaching, encouraging, and passing down wisdom. But in that moment, I needed a wise parent to nudge me back onto the path of wisdom.

This idea of teaching wisdom is sometimes looked down on by those who favor children learning wisdom through experience. And let's be clear: Experience is a much more powerful and lasting teacher than talking ever will be. Lecturing our children is one of the least effective discipline strategies parents have ever invented. Yet there are many times, especially in the early years, when our children have no idea what a wise action might be. By leading them toward wisdom (as opposed to letting them flounder), we're still letting them experience life, but we're not allowing them completely unguided experimentation with the hope that they will figure it out. Children need the wisdom of the adults around them.

Consider the parenting ideal laid out in the book of Proverbs:

Listen, sons, to a father's discipline,
and pay attention so that you may gain understanding,
for I am giving you good instruction.
Don't abandon my teaching.
When I was a son with my father,
tender and precious to my mother,
he taught me and said,
"Your heart must hold on to my words.
Keep my commands and live.
Get wisdom, get understanding;
don't forget or turn away from the words from my mouth.
Don't abandon wisdom, and she will watch over you;
love her, and she will guard you.
Wisdom is supreme—so get wisdom.
And whatever else you get, get understanding."
PROVERBS 4:1-7

A man who has been taught by his father in the ways of wisdom later trains his son in those same ways. We could just as easily talk about a woman taught in the ways of wisdom by her mother who now trains her own daughter in wisdom. Whichever way we mix and match it—fathers and daughters, mothers and sons, blended families, and grandparents—the basic ideal remains the same: wisdom being passed from one generation to the next. This is raising children in the nurture and admonition of the Lord. This is teaching our children what it means to live.

If we're going to point our children down the path of wisdom, where should we look for it? In the Bible, of course! We can scarcely imagine a book more full of wisdom. Yet we don't always read the Bible seeking wisdom. If we look to the Bible primarily as a rule book, a history book, or a science book, we'll regularly struggle to understand it, especially the Old Testament. But when we recognize it primarily as a wisdom book, its treasures open to us in all their beauty.

This is how the book of James describes wisdom for the followers of Jesus: "The wisdom from above is first pure, then peaceable, gentle, open to reason, full of mercy and good fruits, impartial and sincere" (James 3:17, ESV).

This is the kind of wisdom we want to nurture in our kids. This is why parenting in ways that point our children to Jesus really matters. It's not just about parenting that seems effective in the moment; it's about parenting that prepares our children to experience the good fruit of wisdom later. And the way we do that also matters. As James writes just before this: "Who among you is wise and understanding? By his good conduct he should show that his works are done in the gentleness that comes from wisdom" (James 3:13).

Are we parenting in gentleness? It is through gentleness that we show our wisdom. Through my dad's kind and insightful question that day in the car, he demonstrated that he was on the path of wisdom, and he made me want to follow him.

How Do We Help Our Kids Find Wisdom?

One of the family rules in my home when I (Amanda) was a child was "no Bible, no breakfast." Each morning, my brother and I diligently read the corresponding chapter of Proverbs for the day of the month. And by "diligently," I mean I read it as quickly as possible, highlighted the verse that stood out to me (to "prove" I'd read it), and then headed to the kitchen for breakfast.

Those daily proverbs taught me a few valuable lessons. But none of the verses resonated with me quite as much then as they did three decades later when I read Proverbs as a parent. The countless pleadings of a father for his son to heed parental instruction, to seek wisdom, and to hold fast to the teaching of his mother are, in a word, relatable. It takes little imagination to envision an ancient Israelite father sitting at a wooden table after dark, feverishly writing to his son, "Please, please, please pay attention and listen to your parents. We have wisdom to give you if you'll just listen!" It seems as though the prayers of God-following parents haven't changed much in the last three thousand years.

If only wisdom was gained by simply listening to one's parents. Admittedly, as a child reading a chapter from Proverbs every day, I assumed that's how wisdom is acquired. Step one: Read the Bible. Step two: Listen to Mom and Dad. Easy-peasy, lemon-squeezy. A hefty dose of wisdom is served right up!

While Proverbs (and all of Scripture) does provide insight on how to attain wisdom, the book of Ecclesiastes, which I read through as an adult, brought me real-world clarity to this important topic. Can wisdom be learned simply by reading and following directions? Potentially, yes! Yet in Ecclesiastes we see that wisdom is learned, in large part, through experience—through trial and error, through the process of maturing and having lived experiences under your belt, which provide critical context to the probable outcomes of familiar patterns, habits, and situations.

As parents, we have the opportunity to introduce our children to wisdom, not only through our verbal instructions and through reading Scripture to them, but also by allowing them to learn through experiences very early in life. Because we know that children's brains develop slowly, we can expect that guiding them toward wisdom and allowing them to learn through their own experiences will take time. Your job right now isn't to help your children master wisdom. Rather, it is to protect their physical and emotional well-being as they're learning, and to nurture them through the first part of their journey toward wisdom.

There are many ways to do this, and next we'll focus on a few you can practice today, no matter how old your children are.

Choose to give a choice

"The way kids learn to make good decisions is by making decisions, not by following directions," says Alfie Kohn, who writes and lectures widely on education.[1] His words highlight a fundamental truth about decision-making: Practice is key. Children need lots of opportunities to make decisions, even if they make mistakes along the way. Merely following directions and being told what choices to make will hinder their growth and limit their ability to develop crucial decision-making skills and gain wisdom needed for the rest of their lives. Children must actively engage in the decision-making process to learn how to make sound judgments and choices.

When we give children the opportunity to make decisions, we give them the gift of experiencing the consequences of their choices, both good and bad. This hands-on experience allows them to learn from their mistakes, reflect on the outcomes, and adjust their decision-making process accordingly.

Furthermore, learning to make decisions through trial and error helps children develop critical thinking skills and build wisdom. Over time, and with lots of practice, they learn to analyze information, weigh options, and consider multiple points of view before making a choice. Will they be good at this as a two-year-old? Not remotely. They probably won't even be all that great at it at seven or eight. But herein lies beautiful, peacemaking potential: By allowing them lots of practice when they're two or three, they'll have more skills at seven or eight than if you make most of the decisions for them until middle childhood.

Ultimately, critical thinking, good decision-making, and the ability to make wise choices are foundational skills that set children up to flourish in all aspects and at every stage of their lives!

Offer small choices within a big boundary

As we discussed in the chapter on obedience, choices are a great way to empower our children. However, most young kids do not have the cognitive ability to navigate a decision with more than two choices. It takes all of their abilities to think about just two options, and they may still make impulsive decisions. During the toddler and preschool years, you can help grow their wise decision-making "muscles" by offering two choices within a boundary that aligns with your values, goals, and family culture, and of course, that keeps them safe.

- Do you want to put on your shirt first, or your pants first?
- Do you want tomatoes or carrots with your lunch?
- Would you like the orange plate or the purple plate?
- Do you want to read a Bible story or a poem before bedtime?

Encourage big choices with small(ish) risks

The examples above are of small choices that carry no real risk. Admittedly, I (Amanda) struggle with giving my children freedom to take risks, but because I know that allowing them to do so is essential for their growth and development, it is a major focus of my own growth as a parent. When children are given the freedom to experiment and try new things, they learn valuable lessons about themselves, their abilities, and their limitations. By taking risks, children step out of their comfort zones and confront challenges, which helps them learn adaptability and problem-solving skills. It allows them to develop a strong sense of self and boosts their confidence in their abilities to overcome obstacles.

These benefits are often evident to us when we observe our children in nature—their eagerness to climb trees, jump off fallen logs, and explore under rocks brings important learning opportunities.

The benefits aren't quite as obvious when we catch our little ones climbing on furniture to reach a high shelf, experimenting with mixing liquids in the kitchen, or digging through a bathroom cabinet to see what they can find—all of which, while seemingly mischievous, provide opportunities for children to be curious and learn about consequences and problem-solving.

Taking risks also encourages creativity and innovation. Children who are allowed to explore new ideas and possibilities without fear of failure or judgment—and without the threat of their parents stepping in unnecessarily—are more likely to think outside the box and come up with unique solutions. Over time, they'll develop a mindset that embraces experimentation and learning from mistakes. This mindset not only fosters their intellectual and creative development but also prepares them for the uncertainties and complexities of the real world.

Of course, proper supervision, guidance, and age-appropriate challenges are necessary to ensure our children's physical and emotional well-being. As parents, we must utilize our own wisdom to find the sweet spot between providing a safe space and encouraging risk-taking. This way, our children can explore their potential, discover their passions, and develop the skills needed to navigate the opportunities and challenges they will face in the future while staying safe in the present. While it may take a lot of work for us as parents, by staying calm, confident, and willing to be inconvenienced, we empower our children to develop the skills and wisdom that will serve them their whole lives.

Ask questions that lead to the answer

We've all experienced it: Our child is trying something new, and it's taking way longer than it should. A quiet thought runs through our minds: *I'm the adult. I know the best way to do it. Maybe I should just tell them what to do. After all, I know best.* We *are* the adults!

We *do* often know what's best. We do have decades of experience with which to discern the way of wisdom. But when it comes to leading and guiding our children, setting aside the "knower" mindset and choosing to cultivate learning helps us understand our children and their unique needs—and it helps us lead them in learning wisdom. Being curious about our kids' thought processes and asking good questions are ways to encourage them to begin thinking for themselves. That's exactly what I was doing when I talked with our son Ezra about his scooter.

When it comes to asking questions, keep a couple of key points in mind:

- The goal is to guide your kids through a process. Questions that can be answered with just a yes or no should be avoided. Opt instead for open-ended questions.
- Children aren't robots, and they may not give the answer you expect or even want. Asking more questions instead of correcting the "wrong" answer can help them develop the ability to think critically.
- When time allows, continue asking questions until they process all the steps or solve the problem for themselves.
- Children with auditory processing challenges or who are neurodiverse may not respond well to lots of questions. In that case, keep your questions simple, using "What's your plan?" and "I wonder . . ." as neutral ways to guide the conversation.

Not surprisingly, our kids are going to make their fair share of unwise decisions. It is in those moments that we must remember that it isn't shame or blame that leads children to wisdom. On the contrary, the disappointment or frustration that may naturally result should invoke compassion and loving-kindness from us as we help our children learn from poor choices. In the aftermath of such moments, thoughtful, heartfelt questions can help encourage wisdom in the future:

- What could you have done differently?
- What do you think would have happened if you'd made a different choice?
- How can you remember the different choice next time?

Tiny Victory, Big Wisdom

Nine-year-old Ezra, sweaty and dirty, walked in through our back door one evening. I knew that, at his age, it was still a toss-up as to whether or not he'd be stinky. Some days he smelled like dirty little boy—more like a wet puppy than anything else. But other days I questioned whether a full-grown man who'd been working in the heat stood before me. The time between little kid and big kid is full of mystery and surprises, including what they might smell like on any given day!

Ezra was returning from our church's Vacation Bible School, "Rock the Block." With only two years left before he aged out, he was one of the big kids, and each night he came home excited and ready to share about what he'd done and learned.

"Guess what they had to drink tonight?" he asked, his big blue eyes sparkling. I couldn't tell where this was headed. Every other night they'd just offered water, so the exception could be anything from a juice box to soda—either way, he'd have been excited. "Soda?" I guessed.

"Yeah! They had *Dr. Pepper!*" he said with palpable enthusiasm. We're not a zero-sugar family, but in general we do avoid caffeinated drinks, especially in the late afternoon and evening.

"Oh, really?" I said, a bit nervous since it was already past bedtime. He was practically jumping out of his skin, and I silently started preparing myself for a longer and louder than usual bedtime routine.

"Yeah! But guess what?" Ezra said. "I chose to drink Sprite." He was so proud, and inside, I was beaming. David and I hadn't been there to make the decision for him, and Ezra knew there wouldn't have been any punishment or imposed consequence if he had chosen Dr. Pepper. He smiled and said, "I told them we don't drink caffeine that late and I wanted Sprite instead so I wouldn't have a hard time falling asleep."

In that moment, angels might as well have been singing the "Hallelujah Chorus." It may seem like a tiny victory, but knowing that our already-late bedtime wouldn't be thwarted by the rare and treasured Dr. Pepper felt like an absolute miracle. On his own, with his friends choosing whatever they wanted and without any parental guidance, Ezra freely chose the wiser option.

Reflection Questions

1. What piece of wisdom passed down to you during your childhood do you treasure most?

2. What are ways you can partner *with* your children in these growing years, giving them the opportunity to practice and gain wisdom for their future?

3. Think of a recent situation in which your child displayed wisdom. How can you retroactively show them appreciation and pride for that moment?

12

Parenting with Peace

I (Amanda) didn't hear the term nap trapped until well after our boys had outgrown their midday sleep routines, but the first time I heard it I was transported back to the countless hours I'd spent rocking or wearing one (or both) of our boys while they slept. One afternoon in particular stands out. I was sitting in our overstuffed, cozy chair reading yet another parenting book while cuddling a sleeping Elijah. Perhaps it would have been more productive for me to nap with him, but instead I was feverishly flipping through a popular Christian parenting book looking for all the right answers. I'm a "give me the list so I can check off all the boxes" type of person, and that's what I wanted when it came to being a good mother.

I was seeking answers to good questions, with good intentions behind them:

How do I make sure my boys grow up to follow Jesus?
What is the best way to parent toddler boys so they learn to
be good Christian men someday?
What is the right way for Christian parents to discipline
children?

I was growing more discouraged with every book I read. Some
had been written by well-known mainstream authors, while others
were by obscure writers read only by a particular subculture. Some
were incredibly helpful and life-giving; others just didn't sit right
with me. But all had this in common: They promised to hold the
key to raising healthy, well-adjusted Christian kids. By this point
in my reading, I had noticed that there wasn't as much alignment
as I would have liked among the experts' views on the right way to
discipline. Instead, I found that the "proper" methods (whether,
how, and when to spank; how long a time-out should be; how
to use sticker charts and rewards; etc.) were conditioned on each
author's lived experience and area of expertise. The right way to
parent as a Christian seemed dependent not on Christ and His
character, which we are called to imitate, but on the opinions and
experiences of the authors I was reading. Now I was skimming
through another book that could be summed up by "My kids
turned out great, so parent the way I did."

Frustrated, I closed the book and pushed back the hot tears
that were beginning to form. One thing I was certain about was
that I had absolutely no desire to start wiping away tears or sniffing
so as to wake my light sleeper.

The weight of motherhood was heavy on my chest, and I could
feel the ache inside me. *Lord!* I cried out silently, aware that the
secret fears of my heart were known only to Him. *All I want is to
do this well so that these boys chase hard after You and don't hate me
when they are grown.*

And in the quiet, as I rocked my spirited son who was born with fire in his soul, I heard the Holy Spirit whisper to me, *That's not your burden to carry. That's not your job.*

For one passing moment I considered picking up the book again. At least it offered some hope of getting the outcome I wanted. But I knew in my heart it was an empty promise. I knew the Holy Spirit was speaking truth to my worried heart. As a parent, there is not a single action or inaction on my part that will guarantee the outcome I deeply desire for my children. And while the relationship I foster with them now will most likely inform and calibrate the relationship we share in the future, my job as a parent is to walk in faithfulness, abide in Christ, and disciple my children in the way of Jesus.

A Legacy of Peace

Perhaps you, too, are tired of the false promises and the thinly veiled formulas that suggest if you just follow this combination of excellent parenting advice, say a bunch of prayers, and wait eighteen years, out will pop a well-adjusted, Jesus-following young adult of whom you'll be able to echo the words of John and say, "I have no greater joy than this: to hear that my children are walking in truth" (3 John 1:4). You've experienced or observed how traditional methods often come with mixed results, both in childhood and adulthood. And these inconsistencies leave you with a lot of questions and a lot of fear.

Certain parenting methods might seem effective for a book's author and for a friend or two from church, but the approach is not accomplishing anything in your own family. Or perhaps one idea really seemed to connect with your firstborn but doesn't seem to be effective for the second child.

Then there are the parents of adult children. After scrupulously following the teachings of a Christian parenting expert, their most active parenting years are over, but the results may not be what they expected. One child may now be a faithful church member, but another won't have anything to do with organized religion, and the third is ambivalent and apathetic about Christianity. There are mountains of shame ready to be heaped on these parents. They must have parented wrong. They must not have implemented the method correctly. Because if they had, all their kids would be committed Christ followers, right?

Let's just call this what it is—the parenting prosperity gospel. It's not hard to find. Just read the back cover of many Christian parenting books. Even authors who completely reject any hint of the prosperity gospel in their theology may fall into the trap of making unsubstantiated promises about how their parenting methods will result in good, moral, Jesus-loving model citizens.

The frustration we felt after discovering that no one technique is guaranteed to ensure that our kids turn out "right" led us to this conclusion: Parenting with deep, abiding peace isn't about having the right answers and methods. It isn't even about seeing all your best hopes and dreams for your child realized. It's about releasing what we can't control and confidently trusting the One who anchors us to His own divine purposes and peace. It comes from placing Jesus not only at the center of our faith but also at the center of our homes and parenting.

As we come to the end of this journey together, it's time to reflect on what it means to bring peace to the conflict and turmoil within your heart as a parent. Parenting with peace is ultimately about trust. It is the embodiment of your knowledge of and hope in the trustworthiness of Christ. It is holding fast to His faithfulness rather than striving to stay faithful to a parenting paradigm. It is resting in the truth that His plans for your child are good, and He will complete the good work He started in them.

This is the legacy of peace that we're leaving our children: an acceptance that while we don't have all the answers and can't always get it right, even in our imperfections we cling to and deeply trust the One who is perfect. We recognize that He is not triggered by our children's immaturity, flustered by children acting like children, or provoked by their lack of development or skills. Actually, that's how He designed them! His plan is good, and His design is intentional.

A Legacy of Purpose

Parenting is a journey of growth and transformation—not just for our children but for us as well. We acknowledge that there is no perfect way to raise children, and our purpose isn't to raise perfect children. Rather, our purpose as parents is to be intentional in our approach and wholeheartedly follow in the footsteps of Jesus. Our legacy lies not in raising flawless children but in guiding them toward understanding the depths of God's love and grace toward them, and surrendering our best hopes, dreams, plans, and goals for our children to His plan and purpose.

We are leaving a legacy of sacred purpose: our profound trust in Jesus' plan for our children. We recognize that our ultimate role is to be faithful stewards of the precious lives entrusted to us. Our children are not extensions of ourselves; they are unique individuals with their own journeys to walk. Parenting with peace means we must surrender our desires for specific outcomes and instead trust that Jesus has a purpose for each child's life.

What is that purpose? The apostle Paul tells us:

God, being rich in mercy, because of the great love
with which he loved us, even when we were dead in
our trespasses, made us alive together with Christ—by

grace you have been saved—and raised us up with him
and seated us with him in the heavenly places in Christ
Jesus, so that in the coming ages he might show the
immeasurable riches of his grace in kindness toward us in
Christ Jesus. For by grace you have been saved through
faith. And this is not your own doing; it is the gift of
God, not a result of works, so that no one may boast. For
we are his workmanship, created in Christ Jesus for good
works, which God prepared beforehand, that we should
walk in them.

EPHESIANS 2:4-10, ESV

God's plan for our children is a life of good works rooted
in acknowledgment of and gratitude for God's rich love, kindness, and grace. The legacy we leave our children, and our ultimate purpose in parenting them, is for them to experience this
resplendent and unconditional love from us first, as imitators of
Christ.

Actions Speak Louder than Words

We met Natalie through social media. She supported our work for
a few years, and when we announced a membership option, she
was one of the first to join. The oldest daughter of nine children,
Natalie had been raised in a movement of the 1990s and early
2000s that claimed having large families was the biblical way. The
movement had prepared her to parent many small children—or
so she thought.

When she connected with us, she was struggling as a mom of
six children under the age of eight and was trying to disentangle
herself from everything she thought she knew about Christian
parenting. As another mom with several young children lamented,

giving words to Natalie's plight, she felt more like a "chaos manager" than a mother.

Natalie's biggest challenge? Finding the balance between understanding and accepting childish behavior as developmentally normal—and therefore something to be expected and anticipated—and harnessing opportunities to teach and disciple her little ones toward growth and maturity. Like many parents who are breaking harmful parenting cycles, she found herself swinging between being permissive and overly harsh. And just like hundreds, if not thousands, of parents we've talked with, she knew that what she taught her children about God, sin, and grace would be learned more by her witness than her words.

Natalie's father was a pastor, and she understands all too well the confusion and frustration that came from shouldering the unrealistic expectation that she appear perfectly well-behaved and mature beyond her years as "evidence" of her parents' good, godly, and impressive parenting. She, like so many Christian parents today, is deep in the trenches of untangling behaviorism and moralism from trust and faith.

Some parents love to talk about faith with their children. Others are a little less sure how to discuss these subjects with their kids. But overwhelmingly, Christian parents make sure their children hear the good news of Jesus Christ. Of course, telling kids about Jesus is the easy part. Living out the way of Jesus in front of them is the real challenge. If there is a mismatch between our words about Jesus and the lives we live as followers of Jesus, our kids will notice the difference. A three-year-old child may not notice that we're telling them about a God of unconditional love while offering them love primarily when they act in certain ways, but by the time they are thirteen or twenty-three, they will certainly have spotted the disconnect.

In this quest to parent with peace and purpose, we have

endeavored to model Jesus' Kingdom ethic in our home and family by embodying, as best we can, the values He taught us— compassion, forgiveness, humility, empathy, love, grace, and peace. Spiritual and character formation begin not by managing or controlling our children's behavior but by introducing them to the character and heart of Christ. Telling children about God's grace is easy. Actively showing them that grace is what peacemaking parenting is all about. When your children begin to launch into the world, they will have seen grace in action in your home, which will enable them both to receive and give grace to others. Your children will have felt unconditional love and respect, thus enabling them to recognize unhealthy expressions of love and twisted forms of respect, preparing them for healthy relationships throughout their lives. When you lay a foundation of unconditional love in a child's life, that foundation doesn't just encourage a connection with the parent but also benefits many future relationships.

As you cultivate and access the fruit of the Spirit in your parenting, your children will be primed for the work of the Holy Spirit in their own hearts, recognizing that it is neither a passive experience nor a heavy burden of work on their part.

If there is one thing I (David) have learned in more than twenty-five years in ministry, it's that, no matter how much I wish I could, I cannot do the work of the Holy Spirit. I do not have the power to change people's hearts, minds, and lives. It is not my job to convict a person of sin or transgression. And it is not within my ability to grow another person's faith. I can show people the path of following Jesus, I can encourage them to walk in it, and I can be part of the community of faith that helps them when they stumble and struggle, but I cannot compel them to follow Him.

It's no different with our children. What I can do—and what you as a mom or dad can do—is plant and nurture seeds of faith. A parent can plant and water, but ultimately it is only God who can grow faith. Yet when we do this work as part of following Jesus, we're nurturing a faith built on indescribable grace, not punishment.

A Legacy of Experiential Faith

As Christian parents, our relationships with our children are intertwined with our relationship with God. We have the privilege of planting seeds of faith in the hearts of our little ones. And we do this in many ways, including reading Scripture to and with our children, incorporating prayer into the rhythms and routines of our days, and worshiping through music, poetry, art, and song. These are good and appropriate ways to sow those seeds.

But ultimately, if we lay a foundation of holy habits without introducing our children to the character of Jesus, their faith will be one of works-based behavior rather than trust-based obedience to Christ.

It is by living out His teaching in our homes that our children first begin to learn of His goodness and kindness toward them. It is through our embodiment of Christ's Kingdom ethic that our children gain not merely a cerebral understanding or list of facts about God and the Bible but an experiential knowing of what God is like.

When I (David) was a child, I was introduced to a God of grace and love. But that wasn't a foreign concept to me. I knew what grace was because I had experienced grace in my home. So when I listened in church or read my Bible, I intuitively understood some of these biblical ideas about God. My parents weren't perfect, but their love for Jesus was (and is) unmistakable. They laid a theological foundation in my life that still endures. But here's something I've learned after fifteen years as a theology professor— lots of Christians struggle to accept a God of grace and mercy who loves them unconditionally. They have a deep-rooted fear that God loves them only if they behave the right way. If there is one hope I have for my children and yours, it's that they see grace and unconditional love in action so they're prepared to believe in and follow God—not a god of their imaginations or a god of behaviorism and works cloaked in Christian language, but the God who revealed Himself in Scripture.

A Legacy of Unconditional Love

"I remember when I realized my old parenting approach had backfired on me," said one of the moms in our mentorship group on a Thursday night Zoom call. A single mom, Alayna was already aware of the impact her parenting had on her relationship with her eleven-year-old daughter, Olive. However, it was an "out of the mouths of babes" moment that brought instant clarity to how it had influenced her daughter's understanding of God.

Alayna's relationship with her daughter had suffered the stress and trauma of the family dysfunction that led to Alayna separating from her husband. While their relationship was still strained, she was already starting to notice the rebuilding of trust with her daughter.

"I was lecturing Olive about how God gave her talents and gifts for a reason, to bless her and others. I really thought she was starting to get it, but then she looked up at me and said, 'I know that's why God gave them to me, Mom! And I also know He'll take those gifts away when I'm bad. So then what?'" Olive expertly expressed the tween angst and attitude most parents are familiar with.

Our hearts were tender as we listened to Alayna recount that interaction. Most of the families in our mentorship group have younger children, and Alayna's report brought a moment of levity to our connection call. She explained that Olive viewed God as little more than a puppet master, dangling a carrot of blessing in front of her only if she obeyed but ready to take away her natural gifts and talents if she messed up.

This is not the God whom Jesus revealed in His life or death. Jesus demonstrated that God is willing and ready to absorb the sins of His beloved creation so they may flourish in abundant lives of love and service to Him and others, regardless of the specific situations they encounter.

Parenting with peace and purpose leaves a legacy of unconditional love for our children. Not because they earn our favor and love with their behavior, but because they recognize that they are treasured image bearers of God whom He sees as blessings and gifts.

In their book *Discipline That Connects with Your Child's Heart*, authors Jim and Lynne Jackson describe misbehavior as an "irreplaceable golden opportunity" for unconditional love. They explain that if we show our favor, pleasure, and love to our children exclusively when they're well-behaved, we are missing the only opportunity when unconditional love means anything to them: while they're acting in the most unlovable ways.[1] That's why, throughout this book, we have embraced discipline as discipleship rather than punishment.

When I (Amanda) think back to the younger me stealing away whatever minutes I could to search for the secret to raising children who love God and others well, I wish I could reassure her that she was just about to find the path to peace (internal, if not always external) in parenting. Now we invite you to choose grace-based, peacemaking discipline too. As you do, you'll learn to respond to your child with understanding and patience, focus on the heart behind their actions, and address the potential developmental or neurological roots of their behavior rather than merely correcting or punishing their actions or choices. You'll demonstrate the unmerited favor of grace, reflecting God's love for you—and for them.

Reflection Questions

1. What legacy do you want to leave your children? What actions can you take today that will contribute to that legacy?

2. How has your view of and relationship with Jesus changed as you've walked through these chapters? How can you begin to impart that new wisdom to your children?

3. As you consider the journey you've been on in these pages, what are some of your most valuable takeaways? What's one actionable step you can take today as a peacemaker parent?

A Benediction for You

As you conclude this journey, remember that your efforts are not in vain. The seeds you are sowing in the fertile soil of your children's hearts will bear fruit for years to come. Your legacy is not defined by your parenting perfection but by your commitment to follow in the way of Jesus and to trust His Spirit to cultivate the seeds you're diligently planting throughout your children's lives.

May you lean into the trustworthiness of Jesus, finding shalom—whole-person peace and flourishing in His plan for your children's lives. May you continue to grow, learn, and adapt as you walk alongside your children, supporting them in becoming the individuals God created them to be.

And may the legacy you leave behind be a testament to the love and grace of your Lord, Jesus Christ.

Thank you for joining us on this journey of parenting with peace and purpose. May God's abundant blessings be upon you and your family, now and always.

May your home and family flourish,

Amanda and David

Discipline as Discipleship

Quick Reference Guide

Throughout the pages of this book, we've invited you to view parenting as so much more than behavior management and to think deeply about how your theology and faith inform your parenting. And while the heart of parenting with peace is not about having the *right* techniques or formula, we also know that it can feel disempowering to remove tools from your parenting toolbox without replacing them with practical, *peacemaking* approaches. Some of the following ideas have been discussed elsewhere in the book, but you can use this quick reference guide in the more intense moments of parenting.

Do-Over

Ages two and up

Do-overs are a no-pressure way to give a child a second (or third or fourth) chance to do what is expected. Bonus tip: Turn into a playful fairy or robot to offer the do-over as a way to help defuse tension: "Malfunction! Malfunction. Reprogramming. *Beep. Boop.* Do-over sequence initiated."

As children grow and mature, they become more aware of their ability and capacity to choose in the moment, even when they don't want to! Those are the times when giving a do-over is a practical display of grace and kindness. You will need to actively help toddlers and preschoolers with their do-overs. For older kids, a simple, "Please try saying that again with your regular voice" can prompt them to self-correct an unkind tone of voice.

The power of a do-over is amplified when you, the parent, actively model trying again and starting over for your children. When you respond harshly or in a way that does not align with your values, say something like, "Whoops. That's not how I want to respond when you two are fighting. I'm going to try that differently." Then simply respond with the tone of voice and physical posture you want to use, even if you're not quite sure what to say.

Find the Yes
Any age

When we overuse "No" and "Don't" in talking with our children, dozens of stress-producing hormones and neurotransmitters are released in their brains.[1] It's not that we never say no—that isn't realistic—but when it is possible, save "No!" "Stop!" and "Don't!" for urgent and serious situations. Finding the yes literally impacts kids' brains for the better, helps reduce power struggles, and helps our children find an acceptable action they can do.

Some examples:

"Hands in your pockets!" instead of "Don't touch that!"
"Let's go outside to yell" instead of "Don't yell in the house!"
"Use soft hands" instead of "Don't pull the dog's ears."
"Keep the ball on the floor" instead of "Don't throw in the house!"
"Put your bottom on the chair" instead of "Don't stand on the chair!"

"You can chew on this toothbrush!" instead of "Don't put that in your mouth!"
"You may bounce on the exercise ball!" instead of "Stop jumping on the couch!"

Future-Facing Consequences

Any age

Just like with any skill and ability, repetition, failure, learning from mistakes, and trying again are critical parts of the learning process. This goes for so many common behavior struggles! In addition to helping or holding a boundary, get creative with future-facing consequences. Do-overs, role-playing, skill-building games, and memorizing family rules and values through songs and rhymes can all be used to help equip your child to do better next time.

For example, a toddler who consistently hits when they're upset will benefit from practicing having "safe hands." You can modify Simon Says to play a hands-only version to help them learn about being in control of their hands, or you can create a safe-hands zone by tracing their handprints and having them focus their attention on their hands. The big idea here is that because their behavior is developmentally appropriate, you aren't punishing them for it, rather you're finding many ways to reinforce their learning and development of impulse control.

Gentle and Firm Boundaries

Any age; best in early childhood and then done collaboratively within wide boundaries as children get older

Instead of giving arbitrary and unrelated consequences, simply hold boundaries that are not negotiable with gentle firmness. Kindness and firmness are not mutually exclusive! "You are so angry that you want to hit! It's okay to be angry, and it is my job to keep everyone safe. I'm going to hold your hands while you cry."

Give Choices
Any age

Giving choices helps children feel empowered, honors the agency given to them by God, and reminds them that they have autonomy. It also allows them to practice decision-making when risks are low: "It's almost time for lunch. Would you like the purple plate or the green plate?"

In a moment of misbehavior, this might sound like, "The couch is for sitting, but I can see that your body wants to jump right now! Would you like to jump like a rabbit across the floor, or go jump on the trampoline outside?"

How to give choices: Make sure you are genuinely okay with either choice the child makes, and give them agency within a wide boundary. (It's also helpful to offer them two choices that are typically acceptable to them. This isn't "Do you want get ready for bed or do you want the consequences?" This is "Do you want to take a shower or a bubble bath tonight?")

Parents often present choices with more of a negotiating tone, almost inviting a power struggle. Instead, using a calm and confident voice reinforces your commitment to remaining connected *and* holding a limit at the same time.

When to offer a choice: Giving children the opportunity to practice decision-making and use age-appropriate power is a gift you can give them from an early age. Some children (particularly neurodiverse kids) may struggle with choosing or may feel too controlled by your options. They may benefit from collaboration and problem-solving (see page 228). Younger children typically respond well to two simple choices. As they grow and mature, they will begin to recognize that you're still the one drawing the boundary. Rather than accepting their invitation to a power struggle, evaluate your boundary (is it time to widen it?) or consider collaboration.

Help
Any age

Children's brains are designed to learn by both doing and watching. Rather than telling your children, "Pick up your toys or they're going away," get down on the floor with them. Get them started by saying something like, "It's time to put away the LEGOs. Let's start with the yellow ones." Then help them with the task.

Helping your children follow directions may well be one of the most-used tools during the toddler and early preschool years.

How to help: When working with your child, keep your voice and your body calm. You are their mentor, guide, and most trusted influence. You do not prove that you're in charge by controlling your child; you prove that you're in charge by controlling yourself. This is not about forcing a child to physically comply with a demand but about coming alongside them and supporting their learning skills, boundaries, values, and expectations.

When to help: This will vary based on your and your child's personalities, temperaments, and abilities, as well as your spiritual convictions. Some children flourish within consistent structure, so helping them may look like communicating expectations, waiting for them to process what they've heard and evaluate the next step, and then moving alongside them to help them follow through, as in the example above. Children who thrive with wide boundaries may respond better to a combination of helping and giving choices.

Make Them a Shadow
Ages one to five; best between ages one and three

When a child is struggling, rather than isolating them in their room or in a naughty chair, make them your shadow. This simply means that they stay close to you and do things with you while they calm down. You might start by leading them through active calming strategies, but they could also help you in the kitchen, in the flower bed, or with any activity where you can involve them in age-appropriate ways. Making one child your shadow is also a helpful tool when siblings need to be separated.

Playfulness
Up to age seven or eight

Research shows that children learn more quickly through play. When your child is still learning or practicing a skill (like getting dressed or brushing their teeth), approaching it with playfulness helps release tension and teaches them new skills more efficiently! Use a silly voice, turn into a robot, sing every word of instruction, or pretend you don't remember and need *their* help. For an extensive and research-based discussion on this topic, we recommend the book *Playful Parenting* by Dr. Lawrence Cohen.

PREP (Prepare | Role-Play | Explain | Plan)
Any age

Preparing children in advance helps them go into new or infrequent situations with confidence and an understanding of what to anticipate.

"You're going to the eye doctor on Thursday. Here's what you can expect . . ." Use books, videos, toys, and storytelling to get them ready.

PREP is particularly helpful for building new habits and teaching social expectations.

HOW TO PREP

Prepare: Children don't know what to expect in new situations or when they're learning new skills. At most, they likely know broad concepts rather than specific expectations. Prepare them for new schedules, routines, experiences, and situations by giving them information that will ease their transitions. For example, highly sensitive children may have a strong reaction to bell ringers at Christmas, and you can help prepare them ahead of time by letting them know what to expect. You can suggest they consider covering their ears as a way to cope with the sensory overload. Visual routines and social stories are helpful for preparing kids as well.

Role-play: Children learn most effectively through play and repetition. Role-playing is a play-based way to help them learn social expectations, conflict resolution skills, and important family rules. You can help children learn what's expected in a church service by playing church at home. Or use their toys and dolls to play out tricky scenarios that might come up at a birthday party for a friend.

Explain: When kids have loads of questions, it's easy just to answer "Because" or "That's just how it is." During big transitions and new experiences, it is important to help children understand the reasons and answer their whys. It is also helpful to proactively explain the schedule, how they will know when it is time to leave, how they can occupy themselves if they get bored, and any buddy system they will be a part of.

Plan: Having a plan of action for when things go sideways empowers you as a parent to know what to do ahead of time, and it also helps ease anxiety about the unknown for some children. (Other children may feel anxious when given more information, so this is a great time to be attuned to your child's individual needs.) For example, let's say that before you take your child shopping, you explain that you won't be buying any new toys. Even so, they may still have big feelings about that when you're in the store. Be prepared by arriving with a plan to add toys to their wish list. As another example, if your child is potty training, let them know that one of the first things you'll do when you get to the zoo is take them to the bathroom. That way they will know what to expect when they have to go while at the zoo.

Problem-Solving/Collaboration
Ages three and up; best for five and up

Problem-solving is an important skill, and children are primed and motivated to learn it. "We have a problem: You both want to play with the princess doll, and there is only one. Let's find a solution that works for everyone. What are your ideas?" For an extensive and research-based discussion on collaborative problem-solving, we recommend the book *The Explosive Child* by Dr. Ross Greene.

Role-Playing
Ages three and up

As previously mentioned in the PREP tool, role-playing allows children to practice tricky situations or challenging behaviors in low-pressure and neutral moments. Role-playing is often useful on its own as well. Give your children instructions for what you want them to do, and then practice with them by playing pretend and switching roles.

Songs/Music

Any age

Don't worry if you can't carry a tune! Put a tune to important concepts and boundaries to help kids learn through music. "We hold hands in parking lots, parking lots, parking lots! We hold hands in parking lots to keep our bodies safe!" can be sung to the tune of "This Is the Way We Wash Our Clothes."

As children age, they will not benefit from silly songs quite as much as they did when they were toddlers and preschoolers. That doesn't mean you give up singing altogether, though! Redirecting your harsh tone to a soothing tune will actually help regulate your nervous system and will likely gain kids' attention more effectively than getting upset with them.

Storytelling

Any age

Using stories is one of the most powerful ways to teach children. In fact, it's one of the most powerful ways to teach anyone—just look at how many stories Jesus used to teach important lessons! Through storytelling you can help children learn empathy, understand another person's perspective, process hard experiences and feelings, and brainstorm different ways to respond to specific situations. It can also be used to get an inside look at how your child might learn best or how they want you to treat them when they mess up.

How to use storytelling: Create an imaginary character or cast of characters who are relatable to your child. When your little one is struggling with a particular challenge, tell stories about those difficulties. Your story can either reflect on a tricky behavior or be used to prepare your child for an upcoming big or new experience.

Here are a few examples:

- When toddlers are struggling with biting, consider telling a story about Bitty Bear, who bites her friend, Susie Squirrel, because Susie didn't want to play Bitty's game. Share the story from Susie Squirrel's perspective, and then ask, "What could Bitty Bear have done differently?"

- When you as a parent have a rough day and yell or become overly harsh, consider a story about Mama Bear, who has a bad day and roars at Bitty Bear to pick up her toys. Ask, "How do you think Mama Bear should respond next time?"

- When a child is going through a picky food phase, have Bitty Bear experience strong food preferences and normalize having different taste buds, being willing to try something new—even if it is just feeling it at first—and saying "No, thank you. Not this time."

- When you're about to visit extended family, have Bitty Bear prepare for a trip to see Granny and Grampy Bear, and talk about feeling nervous around new people or new spaces.

- When your little one is about to start day care or school, tell a story about Bitty Bear starting school. Imagine what a day at school might look like and normalize feelings of anticipation, excitement, and nervousness.

- When you have an event coming up that requires quite a bit of waiting, imagine Bitty Bear having to wait in a long line or sit through an important meeting, and collaborate on ways Bitty Bear can quietly pass the time.

As children age, imaginative storytelling will give way to wisdom-based, real-life stories from your own childhood or lived experience. Rather than telling your grade-schooler to be kind and respectful at school or co-op, tell a story from your own memory that emphasizes the impact of kindness and respect.

Storytelling takes a child's particular struggle and redirects it to a relatable character (whether imaginary or you, their parent), which allows them to learn without pressure and even helps them with problem-solving.

Time-In
Any age; best for ages one to five

Time-in is a tool that allows a child to co-regulate with their caregiver in a calming corner or quiet space. "I can tell you're really upset. We're going to the calm-down corner, and I will share my calm with you when you're ready." Time-ins are especially helpful for children who have strong emotional responses and who benefit from taking a break when things are escalated.

An important note: Some children, just like some adults, regulate better by moving their bodies! These kids may be strongly averse to time-ins, so persistently pursue wisdom and understanding of your child's specific needs as you learn how best to help them.

Visual Guides/Social Stories
Any age

Visual guides and social stories give a pictorial reminder to children of what is expected. A visual guide can be as simple as taking a picture of what the toy shelf looks like when toys are picked up, or it can be a visual aid you purchase that shows all the steps to getting dressed. Neurodiverse children especially benefit from visual routines that help them see the structure they so often need.

Social stories are stories or short narratives that help kids understand and navigate social situations. They describe a social situation or concept in a clear and structured way and provide information about expectations, routines, and anticipated behavior that can help children prepare for new or tricky situations. You can do an online search for "social stories + specific situation" (for example, social stories + going to the dentist) and find many free videos and printables, as well as books to purchase.

Acknowledgments

Flourishing is so dependent on community. We couldn't have done this without our family, closest friends, and trusted colleagues.

To our parents, Fran and Kelvin and Vera and Murray. Your support, encouragement, and curiosity have been the wings that allow us to fly and the roots that keep us grounded. In spite of traveling your own difficult journeys during the writing of this book, you've stepped in and provided tangible help like picking up the boys from school, cooking us dinner, and creating time and space for us to write even when it wasn't always easy or convenient for you. Thank you for your unwavering love and support, not just during this process but throughout our lives.

Heartfelt gratitude to Jim and Lynne Jackson, cofounders of Connected Families. We are thankful for your mentorship and wisdom in starting a ministry from the ground up. You believed in us before we believed in ourselves, and you've continued to invite us to respond to God's big dreams for us with confidence and humility. Thank you for the legacy you created ahead of us, which paved the way for the work we're doing now. Colaborers in the mission of Jesus, we are so thankful.

To Ruth Buchanan, our writing coach; Jenni Burke, our

literary agent; and Jillian Schlossberg, our editor, thank you for seeing the vision for *The Flourishing Family* when it was still just a dream. You've spoken life and wisdom into our writing and our family, and we're so thankful for your partnership in this project. Ruth, thank you for giving us the tools and encouragement we needed to become authors. Jenni, thank you for championing "live well, work well" on our behalf. Our family has flourished through huge changes and many commitments because of that nugget of wisdom. Jillian, thank you for believing in our message, making a home for it at Tyndale, and stewarding it out into the world.

Flourishing Homes and Families continued to impact families through social media while we wrote this book thanks to our community care manager, Carissa Serrell. Thank you for holding our vision and stewarding it in our absence.

Jason and Tonya, Robyn, Karena, Rachel, and Michelle—your friendship and encouragement have sustained us through one of the biggest accomplishments of our lives. You've listened, celebrated, kept our confidence, fed us, and loved our kids as your own. Thank you for being our people. We're better parents—and now authors—because of you.

Samuel Martin and Drs. Attebery, Parsons, and Hellwig, your thoughtful scholarship and meticulous attention to detail ensured that our work is not only well-crafted but also theologically robust. We are immensely grateful for the invaluable contribution each of you made to this project. Thank you for enriching our writing and editing process with your insight and feedback.

And to the moms and dads who read early versions of our book. Your feedback was invaluable, and we're so excited for you to finally see this finished work!

Notes

INTRODUCTION: FROM FRANTIC TO FLOURISHING

1. Sofie Kuppens and Eva Ceulemans, "Parenting Styles: A Closer Look at a Well-Known Concept," *Journal of Child and Family Studies* 28, no. 1 (2019): 168–181, https://doi.org/10.1007/s10826-018-1242-x.

CHAPTER 1: A GOD-SIZED VIEW OF CHILDREN

1. James R. Edwards, *The Gospel According to Mark, The Pillar New Testament Commentary* (Grand Rapids, MI: Eerdmans, 2002), 306.
2. For the views of children among Greeks, Romans, and Jews, see Ken M. Campbell, ed., *Marriage and Family in the Biblical World* (Downers Grove, IL: InterVarsity Press, 2003).
3. See Matthew 20:16 and 25:40.
4. Allen P. Ross, *Creation and Blessing: A Guide to the Study and Exposition of Genesis* (Grand Rapids, MI: Baker Book House, 1988), 103–104. For more on literary patterns in the Hebrew Bible, see David Dorsey, *The Literary Structure of the Old Testament: A Commentary on Genesis—Malachi* (Grand Rapids, MI: Baker Academic, 1999).
5. John H. Walton, *Ancient Near Eastern Thought and the Old Testament: Introducing the Conceptual World of the Hebrew Bible* (Grand Rapids, MI: Baker Academic, 2006), 203–215.
6. For more on the image of God, see Carmen Joy Imes, *Being God's Image: Why Creation Still Matters* (Downers Grove, IL: IVP Academic, 2023).

CHAPTER 2: THE POWER OF ABIDING

1. We further explain this concept in chapter 6. Suffice it to say, the military and political success of ancient Rome was hard-fought, and a facade of peace was gained through domination and forced compliance.

2. Timothy Keller (@timkellernyc), Twitter post, December 13, 2022, 6:17 a.m., https://twitter.com/timkellernyc/status/1602638728895291394.

CHAPTER 3: CULTIVATING INNER PEACE

1. Two that we found particularly helpful are *Transforming Trauma: The Path to Hope and Healing* by Dr. James Gordon and *Burnout: The Secret to Unlocking the Stress Cycle* by Amelia and Emily Nagoski. While we don't agree with all these authors' presuppositions and positions, their insights into the way our minds and bodies work together have enabled us to parent with more gentleness and grace.

2. There can be any number of underlying issues that influence how sensitive your stress response is, and it is important to seek the counsel and expertise of those who can help you determine and address the root cause.

3. James Leo Garrett Jr., *Systematic Theology: Biblical, Historical, and Evangelical*, 3rd ed., vol. 1 (North Richland Hills, TX: BIBAL Press, 2007), 53.

4. When an Egyptian papyrus containing the Instruction of Amenemope was discovered and then translated more than a century ago, Old Testament scholars first noticed the similarities between Amenemope's sayings and this portion of Proverbs.

5. For more on Agur, Amenemope, Epimenides, and Aratus, see Robert K. Johnston, *God's Wider Presence: Reconsidering General Revelation* (Grand Rapids, MI: Baker Academic, 2014), 71–77, 110–116.

6. For a detailed examination of issues around God, revelation, and science, see Tim Morris and Don Petcher, *Science and Grace: God's Reign in the Natural Sciences* (Wheaton, IL: Crossway, 2006).

7. Emily Nagoski and Amelia Nagoski, *Burnout: The Secret to Unlocking the Stress Cycle* (New York: Ballantine, 2019), chapter 1.

8. James S. Gordon, *The Transformation: Discovering Wholeness and Healing after Trauma* (San Francisco: HarperOne, 2019), 67.

9. John H. Coe and Kyle C. Strobel, eds., *Embracing Contemplation: Reclaiming a Christian Spiritual Practice* (Downers Grove, IL: IVP Academic, 2019), 37–136.

10. The amygdala is a part of the brain that functions as your built-in security system. One of its primary roles is to alert you to anything that might be a danger to you. See Adrienne A. Taren et al., "Mindfulness Meditation Training Alters Stress-Related Amygdala Resting State Functional Connectivity: A Randomized Controlled Trial," *Social Cognitive and Affective Neuroscience* 10, no. 12 (December 2015): 1758–1768, https://doi.org/10.1093/scan/nsv066.

11. For a brief examination of the concept of Sabbath, see Walter Brueggemann, *Sabbath as Resistance: Saying No to the Culture of Now* (Louisville, KY: Westminster John Knox, 2014).

12. Nagoski and Nagoski, *Burnout*, 14.
13. Visit https://flourishinghomesandfamilies.com/page/the-flourishing -family-downloads-and-resources for this and other free resources.

CHAPTER 4: PLAYING THE LONG GAME

1. Lawrence J. Cohen, *The Opposite of Worry: The Playful Parenting Approach to Childhood Anxieties and Fears* (New York: Ballantine, 2013), 17.
2. Daniel J. Siegel and Tina Payne Bryson talk about this in their book *The Whole-Brain Child: 12 Revolutionary Strategies to Nurture Your Child's Developing Mind* (New York: Delacorte Press, 2011).
3. Karl Barth, "The Beginning of Wisdom," a sermon preached in the prison of Basel, July 20, 1958, in Karl Barth, *Deliverance to the Captives*, trans. Marguerite Wieser (New York: Harper & Row, 1961).
4. M. Teresa Cardador, "The Effects of Positive Versus Negative Impact Reflection on Change in Job Performance and Work-Life Conflict," *Frontiers in Psychology* 5 (November 27, 2014): 1370, https://doi.org /10.3389/fpsyg.2014.01370.
5. For the long-term consequences of using fear as a parenting practice, see John David Eun et al., "Parenting Style and Mental Disorders in a Nationally Representative Sample of US Adolescents," *Social Psychiatry and Psychiatric Epidemiology* 53, no. 1 (January 2018): 11–20, https://doi .org/10.1007/s00127-017-1435-4.
6. For a much more thorough exposition of this parable and its relation to parenting, see Scott Keith, *Being Dad: Father as a Picture of God's Grace* (Irvine, CA: NRP Books, 2017).

CHAPTER 5: CREATED FOR CONNECTION

1. Regina M. Sullivan, "The Neurobiology of Attachment to Nurturing and Abusive Caregivers," *Hastings Law Journal* 63, no. 6 (August 2012): 1553–1570, https://www.ncbi.nlm.nih.gov/pmc/articles/PMC3774302/.
2. Ross A. Thompson, Jeffry A. Simpson, and Lisa J. Berlin, "Taking Perspective on Attachment Theory and Research: Nine Fundamental Questions," *Attachment & Human Development* 24, no. 5 (January 24, 2022): 543–560, https://doi.org/10.1080/14616734.2022.2030132.
3. Michael Reeves, *Delighting in the Trinity: An Introduction to the Christian Faith* (Downers Grove, IL: IVP Academic, 2012), 19–62.
4. Hans Urs von Balthasar, "Movement Toward God," in *Explorations in Theology*, vol. 3, *Creator Spirit* (San Francisco, CA: Ignatius Press, 1993), 15–55.
5. Daniel J. Siegel and Tina Payne Bryson, "'Time-Outs' Are Hurting Your Child," *Time*, September 23, 2014, https://time.com/3404701/discipline -time-out-is-not-good/.

6. The phrase *connect before you correct* is popularly attributed to Dr. Jane Nelsen, an author and educator known for her work in the field of positive discipline. While Dr. Nelsen is often credited with popularizing this phrase, it's worth noting that ideas about positive discipline and the importance of connection in parenting and education have been discussed by various authors and experts over the years.

CHAPTER 6: TRUST-BASED OBEDIENCE

1. The apostle Paul does not approve of slavery in his writings, but he does write to churches where both slaves and slave owners were trying to understand how to live faithfully for Christ in a society that rejected the humanity of those made in God's image. In places like Ephesians 6 and the book of Philemon, Paul gently points out how slavery is incompatible with Christian theology and orients early Christians toward the abolition of slavery, which they eventually will do (sadly, more than once).
2. Harold W. Hoehner, *Ephesians: An Exegetical Commentary* (Grand Rapids, MI: Baker Academic, 2002), 720–729.

CHAPTER 7: CULTIVATING RESPECT IN CONFLICT

1. George Markowsky, "Information Theory: Physiology," *Encyclopedia Britannica*, September 19, 2023, https://www.britannica.com/science /information-theory/Physiology.
2. Karyn Purvis and Lisa Qualls, *The Connected Parent: Real Life Strategies for Building Trust and Attachment* (Eugene, OR: Harvest House, 2020), 110.
3. Tina Malti, Joanna Peplak, and Linlin Zhang, "The Development of Respect in Children and Adolescents," *Monographs of the Society for Research in Child Development* 85, no. 3 (August 11, 2020): 77, https:// doi.org/10.1111/mono.12417. Emphasis added.

CHAPTER 8: IDENTIFYING THE ROOT OF MISBEHAVIOR

1. J. B. Stump and Chad Meister, eds., *Original Sin and the Fall: Five Views* (Downers Grove, IL: IVP Academic, 2020).
2. See also the Second London Confession of Faith, a Baptist confession that uses the exact same phrasing. The Belgic Confession uses different language but also differentiates between the corruption of sin and the production of sin (Article 15).
3. For an example of an overrealized view of human sinfulness being applied to children in ways far beyond how the Bible or even Reformed theology speak about it, see Voddie Baucham Jr., *Family Shepherds: Calling and Equipping Men to Lead Their Homes* (Wheaton, IL: Crossway, 2011), 113–121. Baucham refers to children as "a viper in a diaper" in a number of sermons, including "The World, the Flesh, and the Devil" delivered at the 2014 Ligonier National Conference (quote begins at about 29:40) and

"Child Training" delivered to Hardin Baptist Church, Hardin, KY, on November 4, 2007. The fruit of Baucham's view of children is evident in his "Child Training" sermon as he describes children needing to be spanked "five times before breakfast" and approvingly recollects a little girl being spanked thirteen times for the "sin" of being shy.

4. For a clear argument from a Calvinist perspective on how total depravity and childhood innocence are compatible, see John MacArthur, *Safe in the Arms of God: Truth from Heaven about the Death of a Child* (Nashville: Thomas Nelson, 2003).

CHAPTER 9: DISCIPLINE AS DISCIPLESHIP

1. Brett Enneking, "Child Development—The Time-Out Controversy: Effective or Harmful?" Indiana University School of Medicine, February 6, 2020, https://medicine.iu.edu/blogs/pediatrics/child-development-the-time -out-controversy-effective-or-harmful.

2. See, for example, Joan Durrant and Ron Ensom, "Physical Punishment of Children: Lessons from 20 Years of Research," *Canadian Medical Association Journal* 184, no. 12 (September 4, 2012): 1373–1377, https://doi.org/10.1503/cmaj.101314.

3. Melanie J. Woodfield, Irene Brodd, and Sarah E. Hetrick, "Time-Out with Young Children: A Parent-Child Interaction Therapy (PCIT) Practitioner Review," *International Journal of Environmental Research and Public Health* 19, no. 1 (2022): 145, https://doi.org/10.3390/ijerph19010145.

4. Mac Bledsoe, *Parenting with Dignity: The Early Years* (New York: Alpha, 2004), 97; Mac Bledsoe, *Parenting with Dignity* (New York: Alpha, 2003), 188. Italics in the original.

5. David L. Allen, *Hebrews*, vol. 35, *The New American Commentary*, ed. E. Ray Clendenen (Nashville: B&H Academic, 2010), 578–581.

6. How best to translate the Bible has been debated by Christians as far back as the time of the church fathers Jerome and Augustine. The translators of the Septuagint were fallible humans who had assumptions and biases but who also were doing their best to communicate God's Word in a different language. Our interest here is not whether their translation is viable (it is), or whether that translation best reflects the intent of the author of Proverbs (probably not), but how does the author of Hebrews understand this verse and use it in the development of his argument?

7. Paul Ellingworth, *The Epistle to the Hebrews*, volume in *The New International Greek Testament Commentary*, ed. I. Howard Marshall and W. Ward Gasque (Grand Rapids, MI: Eerdmans, 1993), 648–649.

8. Edgar V. McKnight and Christopher Church, *Hebrews–James*, vol. 28, *Smyth & Helwys Bible Commentary*, ed. R. Scott Nash (Macon, GA: Smyth & Helwys, 2004), 291–293.

9. Interpretations of Hebrews 12 that focus on athletic discipline instead of punishment are found as far back as ancient times. See Erik M. Heen and Philip D. W. Krey, eds., *Hebrews*, vol. 10, *Ancient Christian Commentary on Scripture* (Downers Grove, IL: InterVarsity Press, 2005), 213–217.

10. Darrell L. Bock, *Luke*, vol. 2, *Baker Exegetical Commentary on the New Testament* (Grand Rapids, MI: Baker Academic, 1996), 1314–1315.

11. David comes from a long line of men who believe that every man should be able to sew on a button or hem a pair of pants, just as he should know how to use a saw or change the oil in the car. We consider these basic life skills for living as adults and teach them to our boys as they become capable of performing them.

CHAPTER 10: WHAT ABOUT THE ROD?

1. R. Laird Harris, Gleason L. Archer Jr., and Bruce K. Waltke, eds., "1389 רען," in *Theological Wordbook of the Old Testament*, vol. 2 (Chicago: Moody Press, 1980), 585. One caveat is that while a young man was able to be independent of his family, that doesn't mean he necessarily left home.

2. Like many languages, Hebrew is a gendered language. The word for young females (*na'arah*) is not used in the rod verses in Proverbs. Only young males are mentioned.

3. This age range could have been as young as ten but was later codified at age thirteen when a boy became obligated to the Law at his bar mitzvah. The upper end of *na'ar* seems to be between eighteen and twenty years. For more on this, see Joseph Fleishman, "The Age of Legal Maturity in Biblical Law," *Journal of the Ancient Near Eastern Society* 21, no. 1 (January 1, 1992): 35–48.

4. For a comprehensive examination of na'ar, see Carolyn S. Leeb, *Away from the Father's House: The Social Location of Na'ar and Na'arah in Ancient Israel*, Journal for the Study of the Old Testament Supplement Series 301 (Sheffield, UK: Sheffield Academic Press, 2000). See also Ted Hildebrandt, "Proverbs 22:6a: Train Up a Child?," *Grace Theological Journal* 9, no. 1 (1988): 10–14; Lawrence E. Stager, "The Archeology of the Family in Ancient Israel," *Bulletin of the American Schools of Oriental Research* 260 (Autumn 1985): 25–27.

5. This point is covered extensively in Carolyn Leeb, *Away from the Father's House*.

6. R. Laird Harris, "2314 טבש," in *Theological Wordbook of the Old Testament*, 897.

7. Bruce K. Waltke, *The Book of Proverbs: Chapters 1-15, The New International Commentary on the Old Testament* (Grand Rapids, MI: Eerdmans, 2004), 462.

NOTES

8. The use of "back" is clear in Proverbs and cannot be read as a more generic "backside." Hebrew has specific words for body parts, much like English does. If the Holy Spirit inspiring Solomon wished to specify buttocks, He could have done so. He did not. William J. Webb, *Corporal Punishment in the Bible: A Redemptive-Movement Hermeneutic for Troubling Texts* (Downers Grove, IL: IVP Academic, 2011), 35–37.
9. For an in-depth study on this matter, see Webb, *Corporal Punishment in the Bible.*
10. Paul D. Wegner, "Discipline in the Book of Proverbs: 'To Spank or Not to Spank?'" *Journal of the Evangelical Theological Society* (December 2005): 720–728.
11. E. T. Gershoff and A. Grogan-Kaylor, "Spanking and Child Outcomes: Old Controversies and New Meta-Analyses," *Journal of Family Psychology* 30, no. 4 (2016): 453–469, https://doi.org/10.1037/fam0000191.
12. Robert D. Sege and Benjamin S. Siegel, "Effective Discipline to Raise Healthy Children," *Pediatrics* 142, no. 6 (December 1, 2018), https://doi.org/10.1542/peds.2018-3112.
13. Akemi Tomoda et al., "Reduced Prefrontal Cortical Gray Matter Volume in Young Adults Exposed to Harsh Corporal Punishment," *NeuroImage* 47, no. 2 (August 2009): T66–T71, https://www.ncbi.nlm.nih.gov/pmc/articles/PMC2896871/.
14. Jorge Cuartas et al., "Corporal Punishment and Elevated Neural Response to Threat in Children," *Child Development* 92, no. 3 (May/June 2021): 821–832, https://doi.org/10.1111/cdev.13565.
15. Jill Anderson, "The Effect of Spanking on the Brain," Usable Knowledge, Harvard Graduate School of Education, April 13, 2021, https://www.gse.harvard.edu/news/uk/21/04/effect-spanking-brain.
16. Sege and Siegel, "Effective Discipline to Raise Healthy Children."
17. Odelya Pagovich, "Israel," in *International Perspectives on Family Violence and Abuse: A Cognitive Ecological Approach*, ed. Kathleen Malley-Morrison (London: Routledge, 2004).

CHAPTER 11: FOSTERING WISDOM
1. Alfie Kohn, *Unconditional Parenting: Moving from Rewards and Punishments to Love and Reason* (New York: Atria, 2005), 169. Italics in the original.

CHAPTER 12: PARENTING WITH PEACE
1. Jim Jackson and Lynne Jackson, *Discipline That Connects with Your Child's Heart: Building Faith, Wisdom, and Character in the Messes of Daily Life* (Bloomington, MN: Bethany House, 2016), 87.

DISCIPLINE AS DISCIPLESHIP QUICK REFERENCE GUIDE

1. Andrew Newberg and Mark Robert Waldman, *Words Can Change Your Brain: 12 Conversation Strategies to Build Trust, Resolve Conflict, and Increase Intimacy* (New York: Avery, 2012), 24.

About the Authors

David Erickson longs to see God's people recognize that how we live our faith imparts theology to others. Nothing brings this into sharper focus than parenting as our daily lives constantly disciple those who know us best. David previously served as a pastor and spent fourteen years as a theology professor at a Baptist seminary. In 2023 he became president of Jacksonville College, where he guides the faculty and staff in preparing students to lead Jesus-centered lives that transform churches, communities, and the world.

Amanda Erickson is wholly and completely captivated by Jesus. A recovering perfectionist, she has found peace and purpose in the perfect love of Jesus. She's passionate about helping moms be less stressed and angry so they can flourish in their motherhood. This passion was born out of her own experience with postpartum anxiety, rage, and anger. A former foster mom and pastor's wife, Amanda is an artist with a free spirit and can often be found water-color painting, sipping coffee on her front porch swing, making up silly songs for her kids and dogs, and hiking the woods near her home in East Texas.